ENCOUNTERING
GOD

The Pathway to His Presence

D1306451

ENCOUNTERING
GOD

The Pathway to His Presence

by

Bishop Charles E. Blake

ENCOUNTERING GOD: THE PATHWAY TO HIS PRESENCE

ISBN 1-880809-94-X
Printed in the United States of America
Copyright © 2004 by Charles E. Blake

Legacy Publishers International
1301 South Clinton Street
Denver, CO 80247
Phone: 303-283-7480 FAX: 303-283-7536

Library of Congress Cataloging-in-Publication Data Pending

1 2 3 4 5 6 7 8 9 10 11 / 09 08 07 06 05 04

DEDICATION

This book is dedicated to my children:

Kimberly Roxanne Ludlow

Charles E. Blake, II

and

Lawrence Champion Blake

ACKNOWLEDGMENTS

A host of individuals comprise the various organizations of which I am apart. All of them have been helpful to me as I pursue ministry. I want to thank the staff members of West Angeles Church, the First Jurisdiction of Southern California, Church of God In Christ, and Save Africa's Children/The Pan African Children's Fund. These are the people who help me to be effective. Special thanks also to my darling wife, Mae, Bishop Dennis Leonard, Elder Wilfred Graves Jr., and Harold McDougal, who helped to refine my words.

CONTENTS

ENCOUNTERING GOD

By those who come near Me

I must be regarded as holy;

And before all the people

I must be glorified.

Leviticus 10:1-3

INTRODUCTION

Late last summer I was led to speak to my people regarding the Ark of the Covenant and its symbolic significance—both in ancient times and today. As I began to study and pray about the Ark, other important related subjects began to draw my attention and to speak to my heart. Among them were the other furnishings in the Tabernacle, the Tabernacle itself, the High Priest, the other priests, the various sacrifices made in the Tabernacle, and the holy days that were celebrated in relationship to it. I began to sense in my spirit that the Lord would have me to spend a few weeks (possibly even a few months) studying and preaching about these subjects and focusing on their message to us as believers in the twenty-first century. After all, Jesus said that He had come to fulfill the Law, and the Bible affirms that the Old Testament Tabernacle, the priesthood, and the sacrifices served as examples and shadows of heavenly things, and that they were all instituted according to a heavenly pattern (see Hebrews 8:1-5). Surely these ancient traditions had much to reveal to us that would make us more effective Christians in our time.

As I began to study and pray about this theme, I felt that I needed to clarify, as much as I could, what it was that God was attempting to accomplish through the Tabernacle, its furnishings, its leaders, and the activities which took place there. What was the nature of the relationship God was attempting to establish with His people? What was it that He wanted? What motivated Him to reach out to man in this way? What was His objective? What I discovered transformed my life and ministry and blessed our congregation and propelled us together toward the supernatural realm.

Now, for the first time in print, I offer these teachings to a wider audience. My prayer is that all those who read them will encounter the God of Israel, the God of the Golden Candlestick, the God of miracles, and understand more fully the pathway to His presence.

Bishop Charles E. Blake
Los Angeles, California

Chapter One

GOD'S MOTIVE, HIS OBJECTIVE, HIS NATURE, AND HIS PROMISES

(or What You Need to Know About God)

For you are a holy people to the Lord your God; the Lord your God has chosen you to be a people for Himself, a special treasure above all the peoples on the face of the earth. The Lord did not set His love on you nor choose you because you were more in number than any other people, for you were the least of all peoples; but because the Lord loves you, and because He would keep the oath which He swore to your fathers, the Lord has brought you out with a mighty hand, and redeemed you from the house of bondage, from the hand of Pharaoh king of Egypt. Therefore know that the Lord your God, He is God, the faithful God who keeps covenant and mercy for a thousand generations with those who love Him and keep His commandments.

1

Therefore you shall keep the commandment, the statutes, and the judgments, which I command you today, to observe them. Deuteronomy 7:6-9 and 11

Before we can discuss any of the furnishings of the Tabernacle, we must better understand God Himself. It was God who instituted the Tabernacle, so if we can understand Him better, we can better understand what exactly He instituted and why.

In discussing God's motive, or purpose, regarding His relationship with us, we must first pause to consider human relationships. In certain ways, relationships are relationships, and the principles are the same—whether it be a relationship with God or with other people.

THE NEED TO KNOW

In order for us to deal effectively with any person, we need to know our own objectives for dealing with that person, and we need to know the objectives of that person in dealing with us. Everybody who smiles at you and treats you nicely is not seeking a relationship with you. Some people just like to smile. They're nice people. In the same way, not everybody who treats you rudely and harshly is responding to something bad you have done or something they don't like about you. Some people are just rude and harsh by nature. So, it's not always about *you.*

Most people are just trying to get from one day to the next and to handle the relationships and situations they already have. So they don't spend a great deal of time thinking about *you.* Unless you're a very special person, most people won't even want to deal with you.

There will be a few people who *will* want to deal with you. Some will want to be your friends, but others will want to deal with you because of something they desire—a favor, a loan, or some other perceived benefit. There is and has been a tremendous amount of pain and confusion in the world today because people who want a relationship have been dealing with others who only wanted relations (of a sexual nature). If you want a godly, honorable, and righteous relationship, you'll have a terrible time dealing with a person who only wants relations, who only wants to use you and then throw you away.

To deal effectively with a person, you need to understand that person. You need to know their preferences, characteristics, goals, and objectives. You need to ascertain their expectations and their requirements for one who would relate closely to them.

If you are to deal effectively with a person, you also need to be motivated. It's tough to be with a person who mistreats you and doesn't care how you feel or what you think. Relationships require an investment of time and both physical and emotional energy, and you need to have the resources, the capacity, and the attributes that will enable you to deal with the other person.

Some people and relationships just require too much emotional energy on our part. Most of us have enough drama in our lives already without adding more of this type of people to the mix. Dealing with them leaves us stressed out and emotionally exhausted. When we have listened to them tell us who is against them and what bad things have been done to them recently, we usually are sorry we asked in the first place. "Lord, deliver us from such negative people," we pray.

These considerations make it necessary for you to first know yourself, being aware of your own preferences and of your minimum acceptable standards. Then, early on in any relationship, you should reveal and articulate who you are and what you are like to the individual with whom you are considering entering into a more serious relationship.

ELEMENTS ESSENTIAL TO A PROPER RELATIONSHIP

For a proper relationship to develop, one that is lasting and satisfactory, there must be mutual admiration and mutual respect. This is absolutely essential.

Everyone who enters into a relationship, especially a covenant relationship, has expectations and preferences which they expect the other party to meet, even requirements which they would impose on the other party. It is very wise to ascertain the expectations and requirements of the other party prior to committing to the relationship.

> *Caring communication is very important in any relationship.*
>
> ◈

It is also necessary to make a prayerful and godly decision as to whether you can and should meet or exceed these expectations and preferences. If you should not or cannot, then you need to either convince the other person to change their expectations or you need to walk away from the relationship before it goes any further. It is always important to do what God wants, not what people want.

Jesus' disciples learned this lesson:

But Peter and the other apostles answered and said: "We ought to obey God rather than men." Acts 5:29

More of us need to learn to walk away from situations that are not convenient to us as Christians. Just walk away! You're better off alone than hanging out with the wrong people, and if you make the mistake of hooking up with the wrong person, you will soon wish you *were* alone. The wise writer of the Proverbs declared:

It is better to dwell in a corner of a housetop, than in a house shared with a contentious woman. Proverbs 25:24

How much more clear do we need to be?

It is unfortunate that so many fail to consider fully the responsibility involved in relationships. They rush into a relationship, having no knowledge of what they are getting into, and, once they get into that relationship, either one party won't express what they want and expect, or the other does not care, will not listen, and/or will not respond. Relationships that are deficient in these areas are doomed to much unhappiness and ultimate failure.

In relationships, people need to talk, and people need to listen. Caring communication is very important in any relationship. There are some who say, "I'm not going to talk. If he [or she] does not know what I want and need, I'm out of here." And there are others who say, "I'm not going to listen. I'm not going to change the way I am or the way I behave." If you have either of these attitudes, you can expect perpetual solitude, constant conflict, and great sorrow in your future. Some couples (even friends) have a big ugly orangutan of a problem sitting right up in the middle of their relationship, but they refuse to recognize that it's there, and they won't even talk about it.

GETTING TO KNOW OTHER PEOPLE

It is impossible for you to just look at people and know what is in them. In the same way, no one can just look at you and know what is in *you*. To really know a person and please them, first, they must tell you about themselves, and you must really listen to them. And, for the people in your life (or the people who want to come into your life) to really know you, you must share openly and honestly with them, and they must listen to you as you do it.

Many married couples have a wall of resentment built up between them. Their homes are like halls of silence because they have failed and continue to fail to communicate effectively. If that's you, you have to start all over again. And you have to try and try again to communicate. And then you have to try some more. Don't stop trying until you get it right.

Then, once you are communicating, you have to sit down and work out the areas of disagreement and conflict and let God bring you into a harmonious and whole marriage. And He can do that.

GETTING TO KNOW GOD

If we want to get to know God better, much of what we consider when entering into human relationships can also apply to our relationship with Him. Down through history, His purpose, motive, and objective, and His nature and promises regarding His relationship with mankind have remained the same. It has been our sins, our limitations, and His knowledge of the proper timing of events that have caused God to deal with mankind in different ways during different seasons.

The matters we will be discussing in this volume fall within the Mosaic dispensation, or dispensation of the Law. As a background to that period, we need to remember again that after four hundred years of slavery, God delivered the children of Israel from Egypt. This was, in essence, their introduction to Him.

This introduction was significant because for four hundred years they had been under the influence of Egypt. That's a very long time, and with the passing of many generations, most memories handed down about their loving God had been erased from their minds.

Even Moses himself knew very little about God, so little that he was forced to ask God by what name he should call Him. Moses had to become acquainted with God and learn how to deal with Him. Then he would have to teach the people to do the same.

All of us have a lot to learn about God. The more we learn, the better it will be for us as God's children, and the more we learn, the easier it will be to receive the miracles we need from Him. So, it's worth the effort. Before proceeding, let us consider four things about our God: His Motive, His Objective, His Nature, and His Promises.

Every dispensation of time began with God approaching man, initiating the action, reaching out to His fallen creature to lift him up. It was no different in the time of Moses. He was surprised by the burning bush and the God who spoke to him through its flames.

When God later spoke to him about building a wilderness tabernacle and told him explicitly how to go about it, how to furnish such a building, what the people were to do there, and who was to administer those activities, He had something very special in mind. Let us see if we can discover together exactly what it was. What was God thinking in that moment?

GOD'S MOTIVE

The answer to our question is given very forcefully in Moses' retelling of the incident as we quoted it for our verse at the beginning of the chapter. God's motive in all of this was clear. It was love:

The Lord did not set His love on you nor choose you because you were more in number than any other people, for you were the least of all peoples; but because the Lord loves you, and because He would keep the oath which He swore to your fathers, the Lord has brought you out with a mighty hand, and redeemed you from the house of bondage, from the hand of Pharaoh king of Egypt. Deuteronomy 7:7-8

"BECAUSE [HE] LOVES YOU"! This truth has the power to change your life.

Why does God speak to us or deal with us at all? Why does He even want to be involved with our lives? Why does He desire to develop a relationship with us? What is His motive? It's simple. God is in love with us.

When you really fall in love, you will not be able to fully explain it, and others will never really understand it. You will overhear some saying things like, "She's lost her mind; I don't know what she sees in him." Love is inexplicable, and when people say, "I love him [or her]," what more needs to be said? Love changes everything.

Parents fall in love with their newborn babies. When a mother or father first holds that tiny infant in their arms, it's love at first sight. They are so much in love that they wouldn't take a million dollars for that child. Love is just that powerful.

God's love for us is like that. Jeremiah wrote:

The Lord has appeared of old to me, saying: "Yes, I have loved you with an everlasting love; Therefore with lovingkindness I have drawn you." Jeremiah 31:3

Just as we are unable to understand the love some people have for each other, we are also unable, at times, to understand what God sees in certain persons—or even in ourselves. Yet He loves us. He doesn't base His love for you on some characteristic or trait that you possess. It's not about the assets that you have. He just loves *you*, and His love for you is everlasting and unconditional. His Word declares it most eloquently:

> *For God so loved the world* [and that most certainly includes you] *that He gave His only begotten Son, that whoever believes in Him should not perish but have everlasting life.* John 3:16

It doesn't matter who you are, and it doesn't matter what you have done: God loves you. I can state this without any doubt whatsoever and put it in writing, because I know it to be true. Our God has proved it over and over again. The songwriter Andrae Crouch has penned:

> *I don't know why Jesus loved me.*
> *I don't know why He cared.*
> *I don't know why He sacrificed His life.*
> *Oh, but I'm glad, so glad, He did.*

You may not understand it, but God loves you. That is the motive for absolutely everything He does in your life.

GOD'S OBJECTIVE

Now that we know God's motive, we must understand His objective. What does He have in mind for you?

God would answer for Himself, "I want to enjoy you, and I want you to enjoy Me. I want to be around you. In fact, I want us to be together forever."

God is not nearly as interested in your regular church attendance and your participation in church activities as He is in the fact that you love Him and He loves you, that you enjoy Him and He enjoys you. This is His objective.

We humans are somewhat displeased when someone we love is suddenly busy with other things and neglects us. We see them looking at something else and talking about something else, and we want to shout, "Hey, I'm here! Give me your attention! Please! I need you to show me your love!" Well, God feels exactly the same way about us, and it's because He loves us so very much.

We are mistaken when we think that God is always demanding things of us.

The psalmist understood this great truth:

Let them shout for joy and be glad, who favor my righteous cause; and let them say continually, "Let the Lord be magnified, who has pleasure in the prosperity of His servant." Psalm 35:27

For the Lord takes pleasure in His people; He will beautify the humble with salvation. Psalm 149:4

God has an abundant plan for everyone whom He calls. He wants you to be blessed, to have the very best life has to offer. Jesus Himself said:

The thief does not come except to steal, and to kill, and to destroy. I have come that they may have life, and that they may have it more abundantly. John 10:10

That's all God wants for you—*"life ... more abundantly."*

We are mistaken when we think that God is always demanding things of us. What could we possibly give to Him that He doesn't already have? When He encourages us to worship Him, it's not that He lacks something. Rather He wants *us* to be blessed as we enjoy Him and He enjoys us.

A father often stands or sits in awe in an infant's room, listening quietly to the rhythmic breathing of his little one, watching the rise and fall of the tiny chest as the baby lies sleeping in the crib. That child is doing nothing at all, but the father loves him or her so much that it doesn't matter. He stays there for an extended period, just enjoying bone of his bone, flesh of his flesh, and blood of his blood, a life that he is responsible for, someone whom he loves so very much and enjoys being around.

When you really love someone, you can sit and look into their eyes for the longest imaginable time. You can sit and hold the telephone, saying absolutely nothing, but being content knowing that someone you love is on the other end of the line.

God is not a demanding God at all. Most parents don't really want anything *from* their children; they just want their children to do well and succeed. Above all, they want their children to be happy and prosperous. Their great despair comes when, after they have invested so much into their children, they see them wasting their lives. That's what hurts a parent.

God's not demanding something from us. His objective is to love us and to be loved by us. He said to the people of Israel through Moses:

Hear, O Israel: The Lord our God, the Lord is one! You shall love the Lord your God with all your heart, with all your soul, and with all your strength. Deuteronomy 6:4-5

Fall in love with God and begin to enjoy a love relationship with Him. Learn to articulate your love for Him, not just in the context of public worship, but also in the privacy of your own home—or anywhere else you happen to be. Don't be afraid to praise Him on the streets of your city. Tell Him, "Lord, You're so wonderful. You're so good, so great. How good it is to be in Your presence! How good to know You."

Praise Him, worship Him, and magnify His name. That's what He longs for. Open your mouth and don't be afraid to let others know that you're in love with Jesus. That's what He is waiting for. More than anything in this world, He desires your expressions of love to Him.

So, God's motive is love, and His objective is to enjoy us and for us to enjoy Him.

GOD'S NATURE

Now, let's go further and look briefly at God's nature. There is much to learn about the nature of God, but we will touch on just a few important points that directly relate to the subject of this book.

As humans, our individual nature determines how people relate to us, and we must understand God's nature if we are to relate to Him properly. Whatever we do, we cannot afford to be disrespectful to God.

Some people are very disrespectful (to anyone and everyone), so disrespectful that we are sometimes forced to say to them: "Listen, I love you, and I'll do almost anything for you, but I simply can't deal with your disrespect. I'm not some kind of flunky or a doormat that you can just walk all over me. You cannot go on talking to me like I'm some kind of dog. I need some respect from you."

God has let us know that if we are to have a relationship with Him, we need to know who He is, and we need to respect who He is. He says to us today, "I love you, and I will do anything for you, but there are some things you need to know about Me. Number one: you need to know that I'm holy."

The Hebrew word used to indicate God's holiness refers to His absoluteness, majesty, and awfulness (or awesomeness) in comparison to us. He is to be reverenced and venerated as totally separate from all that is human and earthly. His holiness refers to His essential and absolute moral perfection.

But God's holiness has not only to do with righteousness, as we often understand it; it has to do with otherness, or specialness. God says, "I'm something else. I am beyond and above anything or anyone else you will ever deal with. I'm different. Nothing and nobody is like Me."

When Moses first approached God on the back side of the desert, He told Moses that He wanted him to come close, but that he would have to take off his shoes in order to approach Him. Where God was represented a very special place (see Exodus 3:5). Moses was not dealing with just anyone; he was dealing with the Lord God, Creator of heaven and earth. Therefore, the shoes had to come off.

Our God is the most high God. When Isaiah saw Him, He was *"high and lifted up"* (Isaiah 6:1), and angels were flying to and fro crying out:

Holy, holy, holy, is the Lord of hosts; the whole earth is full of His glory. Isaiah 6:3

John saw the twenty-four elders casting their crowns down before the Lord and crying out:

"You are worthy, O Lord, to receive glory and honor and power; for You created all things, and by Your will they exist and were created." Revelation 4:11

God is holy, so although He loves us as His children, we cannot deal with Him just any old way. We must relate to Him according to His holiness, according to His majesty, according to His honor.

The fact that God is holy does indeed mean that He is righteous:

You are of purer eyes than to behold evil, and cannot look on wickedness. Habakkuk 1:13

And our holy, righteous God has commanded us to take on His holiness:

As He who called you is holy, you also be holy in all your conduct, because it is written, "Be holy, for I am holy." 1 Peter 1:15-16

Pursue peace with all people, and holiness, without which no one will see the Lord. Hebrews 12:14

In other words, we are not to bring our mess of sin into the presence of the holy God. If we want to have a relationship with Him, it will have to be based on His righteous nature.

God is also a jealous God. His very first commandment to the children of Israel was this:

You shall have no other gods before Me. Exodus 20:3

God told the people, in no uncertain terms, of His jealousy, even naming Himself *"Jealous"*:

For you shall worship no other god, for the Lord, whose name is Jealous, is a jealous God. Exodus 34:14

If somebody tells you that they're jealous, you'd better believe them—especially if they are really tough. And no one is tougher than God; He doesn't take any foolishness. Because He is jealous, when we want to be with Him, then we have to be with Him and no other. We can't be with Him and with the world at the same time. We can't be with Him and with the devil. We can't be with Him and love and serve other gods. And if we are going to be with God, we must obey Him:

If you love Me, keep My commandments. John 14:15

Many have made the mistake of underestimating God, of not respecting His holiness, His righteousness, and His jealousy, and they have paid the price for it.

Because God is holy and jealous, we would all be in serious trouble if He were not also a merciful God:

But the mercy of the Lord is from everlasting to everlasting on those who fear Him, and His righteousness to children's children, to such as keep His covenant, and to those who remember His commandments to do them. Psalm 103:17-18

13

Praise the Lord! Oh, give thanks to the Lord, for He is good! For His mercy endures forever. Psalm 106:1

If it were not for God's mercy, none of us would qualify for His blessings. We would, as the prophet Jeremiah put it, be *"consumed"*:

Through the Lord's mercies we are not consumed, because His compassions fail not. They are new every morning; great is Your faithfulness. Lamentations 3:22-23

Thank God for His mercy. It is forever. The grace of the Lord is forever. The songwriter Frank Williams has said:

> *Your grace and mercy brought me through.*
> *I'm living each moment because of You.*
> *I want to thank You and praise You too.*
> *Your grace and mercy brought me through.*

Grace woke you up this morning, grace started you on your way, and grace enabled you to survive until this very moment. If it had not been for the grace of God, you would not be alive walking on the face of the earth. God had mercy on you and extended His grace to you, that *"amazing grace that saved a wretch like me,"* as John Newton wrote. *"I once was lost, but now I'm found. Was blind, but now I see."*

God's motive is love, His objective is to enjoy me and have me enjoy Him, and I can do it because of His loving and merciful nature. When I throw myself on the mercy of God, He does some wonderful things for me.

GOD'S PROMISES

We cannot close this chapter without talking briefly about the promises of our God. They are, indeed, numerous, and they are wonderful because they are not like the promises of any man. What God promises, He is *"able to perform,"* as Abraham learned:

He [Abraham] *did not waver at the promise of God through unbelief, but was strengthened in faith, giving glory to God, and being fully convinced that what He had promised He was also able to perform.* Romans 4:20-21

Grace woke you up this morning, grace started you on your way, and grace enabled you to survive until this very moment.

God's promises are *"yea"* and *"amen"*:

For all the promises of God in him are yea, and in him Amen, unto the glory of God by us. 2 Corinthians 1:20

If God said He would do it, then He *will* do it. And what has He said He will do for those who enter into a loving relationship with Him? Well, that subject could fill many books. So, let us look at just one important passage of scripture, and see (from the words of Moses) what the promises of God are for your life. Open your heart to every one of these promises:

Now it shall come to pass, if you diligently obey the voice of the Lord your God, to observe carefully all His commandments which I command you today, that the Lord your God will set you high above all nations of the earth. And all these blessings shall come upon you and overtake you, because you obey the voice of the Lord your God:

Blessed shall you be in the city, and blessed shall you be in the country.

Blessed shall be the fruit of your body, the produce of your ground and the increase of your herds, the increase of your cattle and the offspring of your flocks.

Blessed shall be your basket and your kneading bowl.

Blessed shall you be when you come in, and blessed shall you be when you go out.

The Lord will cause your enemies who rise against you to be defeated before your face; they shall come out against you one way and flee before you seven ways.

The Lord will command the blessing on you in your storehouses and in all to which you set your hand, and He will bless you in the land which the Lord your God is giving you.

The Lord will establish you as a holy people to Himself, just as He has sworn to you, if you keep the commandments of the Lord your God and walk in His ways. Then all peoples of the earth shall see that you are called by the name of the Lord, and they shall be afraid of you. And the Lord will grant you plenty of goods, in the fruit of your body, in the increase of your livestock, and in the produce of your ground, in the land of which the Lord swore to your fathers to give you. The Lord will open to you His good treasure, the heavens, to give the rain to your land in its season, and to bless all the work of your hand. You shall lend to many nations, but you shall not borrow. And the Lord will make you the head and not the tail; you shall be above only, and not be beneath, if you heed the commandments of the Lord your God, which I command you today, and are careful to observe them. Deuteronomy 28:1-13

Those who choose to walk with our holy, righteous, just, but merciful God can expect to be filled up with His blessings. He said:

For I know the thoughts that I think toward you, says the Lord, thoughts of peace and not of evil, to give you a future and a hope. Jeremiah 29:11

God says to you today, "I've got good things in mind for you."

He's already blessed you. Just look back to where you used to live and then see where you're living now, and you'll realize it. You used to drive an old car that was practically held together with bailing wire. The tires had so many patches on them that they were just one big patch. Now you're driving something better.

Surely you can remember the time when you had only one suit or one good dress in the closet. Now you have several closets full of clothes. The Lord has blessed you, but that's just the beginning. God wants to take you where you've never gone before.

That's why He's in your life. That's why He's pleading with you right now. That's why He's reaching out to you at this very moment. He wants to give you a future. He wants to give you hope and bless you beyond your wildest imagination. He loves you and extends His mercy to you today.

God is calling you into the Holy of Holies, to the Mercy Seat that was over the Ark of the Covenant there. As we will see in the coming pages, that wasn't possible in Old Testament times, but Jesus took care of all that. He made a way for you to come into the very presence of the living God and to enjoy a divine encounter.

We ought to thank God, praise Him, and give Him glory. We ought to love Him and serve Him, for He is ready to show us the steps necessary to experiencing a divine encounter. Let's get started right now.

Chapter Two

UNDERSTANDING HOLY PLACES, HOLY OBJECTS AND HOLY ACTS

(Or God's Terms of Engagement)

And let them make Me a sanctuary, that I may dwell among them. According to all that I show you, that is, the pattern of the tabernacle and the pattern of all its furnishings, just so you shall make it. Exodus 25:8-9

Before we turn to the articles of interest in the Tabernacle and begin to take the necessary steps toward divine encounter, we must pause and consider the whys and wherefores of holy places, holy objects and holy acts. We are about to look at the basic objects, or pieces of furniture, that were located in the Tabernacle, and it will surely occur to many readers that every item we study will be just that—an item, a thing. Amazingly, the status of the people of Israel with God and His response to them were related to how they dealt with these items, these things, located in the wilderness Tabernacle. Why was this so? Why, in their attempt to rise to the realm of the Spirit, did God require them to deal in this way with material things?

As we shall see in the coming chapters, each of the items was symbolic of something else, or it represented some action.

THE IMPORTANCE OF CERTAIN INANIMATE OBJECTS, GEOGRAPHICAL LOCATIONS, AND PHYSICAL ACTS

All of these items of furniture for the Tabernacle were made from wood and metal, and there was nothing innately sacred or spiritual about the materials from which they were constructed. Why would God use materials like these in the process of our spiritual pursuits? Why would God say, "On your way to Me, you must deal with these tangible inanimate objects, these things"?

And then there is the mystery of the places God used, physical, geographic locations on the face of the earth. As we will see, for example, Moses had to do something special when he found himself approaching *"holy ground"*:

> *So when the Lord saw that he turned aside to look, God called to him from the midst of the bush and said, "Moses, Moses!" And he said, "Here I am." Then He said, "Do not draw near this place. Take your sandals off your feet, for the place where you stand is holy ground." Exodus 3:4-5*

God said that Moses was on *"holy ground,"* and yet it was just a spot on earth that Moses had come upon. Other than the fact that a bush was burning but was not consumed, this place did not look all that different from any other place.

The Tabernacle and, later, the Temple, were also considered to be "*holy*" places. In both of them, there were spots considered even holier:

> *And the holy garments of Aaron shall be his sons' after him, to be anointed in them and to be consecrated in them. That son who becomes priest in his place shall put them on for seven days, when he enters the tabernacle of meeting to minister in the holy place.* Exodus 29:29-30

> *And you shall hang the veil from the clasps. Then you shall bring the ark of the Testimony in there, behind the veil. The veil shall be a divider for you between the holy place and the Most Holy. You shall put the mercy seat upon the ark of the Testimony in the Most Holy.* Exodus 26:33-34

Is not one physical place just like any other physical place? What causes one place to be so different from another one? They're just places.

So there were things and places that were important to God, and there were also physical actions carried out by human bodies that impacted the realm of the spiritual. For example, if the priests had failed to properly wash themselves before entering into the Tabernacle, they would have been killed.

Do we spank our children for not washing their hands correctly? Imagine such a thing! That would seem to be much too severe, and yet God proclaimed the death penalty over those who washed improperly in the Tabernacle. Physical things and physical actions were so important to God that using them properly or doing them properly could mean the difference between life and death.

This is what happened to Nadab and Abihu, sons of Aaron, when they presented to God what the Bible calls "*profane fire*" (Leviticus 10:1). But is fire not fire? And once it is burning, can we tell where it came from? Nadab and Abihu failed to use the fire that God had started, and they suffered the consequences, dying by the hand of God, consumed by fire that fell from heaven. This was serious business. But what was God saying by all of this?

Immediately following this strange event, Moses said something very important to his brother Aaron, something that each of us must get down deep in his or her spirit:

Then Moses said to Aaron, "This is what the Lord spoke, saying: 'By those who come near Me I must be regarded as holy; and before all the people I must be glorified.' " Leviticus 10:3

This is our answer. If we apply it to the first case, we can see that it makes sense. When Moses was in the presence of holiness, he had to remove his shoes. It was because he was in the presence of God that he was standing on holy ground. That's why one place was different from another place; God had chosen to manifest His presence there. And just as a place becomes holy because God is there, things that God chooses to use for His glory are holy, and actions that He ordains us to carry out as indications of our love to Him and our willingness to do His will are also holy.

In what He spoke to Aaron through Moses, God was making two points: (1.) *"By those who come near Me I must be regarded as holy"* and (2.) *"Before all the people I must be glorified."*

In Chapter One, we saw that it is important to understand God if we are to deal with Him successfully, and the first thing we said about Him was that He is holy. God is different. He is special. There is none other like Him inside or outside of our universe. He is the King of the Universe. He is God of all and above all.

Our God is "bad," and by that I don't mean that He's "bad" bad. I mean that He's tough. You don't want to fool around with God. Don't play with Him because He's Holy. He must be respected. He not only wants it; He demands it.

I stated that God is also a jealous God. When God says that He is jealous (and, in fact, that His very name is Jealous), then you need to believe Him. Don't mess with God, for He won't take any foolishness.

God is righteous and just, but He is also merciful and forgiving to those who will seek Him according to His plan.

GOD REQUIRES PRAISE OF THE HIGHEST TYPE

God's nature, as the Most High God, mandates that He be praised, and that His praise be of the highest type. As we will see in Chapter Seven, the mixture of incense that God prescribed for the Golden Altar of Incense was to be used only for Him and for no one else. The same was true of the holy anointing oil. That particular mixture of spices was to be used only in the Tabernacle, nowhere else, and for no other purpose. It was reserved for God alone. God is saying to us that nobody and nothing should receive the same attention and praise we give to Him. Praise Him like you have never praised anyone before.

> *God's nature, as the Most High God, mandates that He be praised, and that His praise be of the highest type.*

God has preferences, as each of us has—especially in reference to the very special person in our lives. If you have a spouse, make sure you know how your spouse wants to be treated, and, within reasonable limits, treat him or her that way. If you don't, there will be someone else waiting in line to do it. And if you're not yet married, your time is coming. Be patient.

In His Word, God has told us how He wants to be treated by His beloved. For one thing, He will be the one making the decisions. God makes the rules, and He sets the terms of engagement. We can't worship Him any way we want to; we must worship Him as He wants to be worshiped.

True worship begins with the heart:

But the hour is coming, and now is, when the true worshipers will worship the Father in spirit and truth; for the Father is seeking such to worship Him. God is Spirit, and those who worship Him must worship in spirit and truth. John 4:23-24

Although there are many processes to be considered and steps to be taken in our worship of God, He always starts with our hearts. If the heart is right, then the rest will come:

O Lord, You have searched me and known me. You know my sitting down and my rising up; You understand my thought afar off. You comprehend my path and my lying down, And are acquainted with all my ways. For there is not a word on my tongue, but behold, O Lord, You know it altogether. Psalm 139:1-4

Search me, O God, and know my heart; try me, and know my anxieties [thoughts, KJV]; *and see if there is any wicked way in me, and lead me in the way everlasting.* Psalm 139:23-24

The writer of Hebrews explains:

For the word of God is living and powerful, and sharper than any two-edged sword, piercing even to the division of soul and spirit, and of joints and marrow, and is a Discerner of the thoughts and intents of the heart. And there is no creature hidden from His sight, but all things are naked and open to the eyes of Him to whom we must give account. Hebrews 4:12-13

When Samuel was searching for a king for Israel, the Lord said to him:

For the Lord does not see as man sees; for man looks at the outward appearance, but the Lord looks at the heart. 1 Samuel 16:7

Moses understood this principle:

And it shall be that if you diligently obey My commandments which I command you today, to love the Lord your God and serve Him with all your heart and with all your soul ... Deuteronomy 11:13

Since God knows the heart, we cannot fool Him on this point. So what must we do? The writer to the Hebrews gives us this powerful admonition:

Let us draw near with a true heart in full assurance of faith. Hebrews 10:22

What the Bible is saying to us is that physical action in the absence of spiritual authenticity—no matter how enthusiastic it may be—is useless and even insulting to God. Your heart has to be right before the rest can come. So when God said, *"By those who come near Me I must be regarded as holy; and before all the people I must be glorified,"* what was He saying? He was saying that we have to treat Him like He's special.

THE IMPORTANCE OF PUBLIC WORSHIP

Like us humans, God especially enjoys being praised publicly, in the hearing of a crowd—*"before all the people I must be glorified."* Few things are more painful than to have a loved one say something bad about you in a crowd, and few things are more gratifying than to have a loved one praise you and say good things about you in the hearing of a crowd.

Jesus taught us that if we are ashamed of Him before men, He will be ashamed of us before the Father:

For whoever is ashamed of Me and My words, of him the Son of Man will be ashamed when He comes in His own glory, and in His Father's, and of the holy angels. Luke 9:26

When we are in a crowd, we tend to be overly conscious of the fact that others are looking at us, and we therefore adjust our manner of worship to something we deem more acceptable to everyone present. Because of this, one of the first things we need to do is to forget about anyone else in the room who might be looking at us and concentrate on worshiping God as He deserves to be worshiped.

When people look at you in church, let them see you, not on some sort of ego trip, but genuinely worshiping God. Forget cuteness and sophisticated articulation. Praise God and praise God alone. He wants to be seen, so He doesn't want *you* to be seen: *"before all the people I [GOD] must be glorified."* Let this be the guiding principle in all of your worship.

THE IMPORTANCE OF GETTING PHYSICAL

If God is to be glorified *"before all the people,"* then we must become physically active for Him. Without that, the people around us will have no idea what we are doing. Without the physical, there is nothing to see.

Unless God can impact us at the level of the physical, He cannot impact us at the level of the spiritual.

Physical behavior matters much to God, just as it does to each of us. None of us would be happy with a loved one who gave us only thoughts, but not words, or words and no actions. We all want more than thoughts and more than words.

We *want* words, and words are wonderful, but we still want more. We want physical actions, and so we expect good deeds and acts of kindness and affection from those we love. In the same way, God expects good deeds and acts of kindness and affection from those who claim to love Him. You have to *do* something.

Unless God can impact us at the level of the physical, He cannot impact us at the level of the spiritual. The Bible is filled with words about bodily, physical behavior—in relationship not only to worship, but also to moral living, in relationship to other people, in relationship to money and material things and much more. For example, Paul wrote:

> I beseech you therefore, brethren, by the mercies of God, that you present your bodies a living sacrifice, holy, acceptable to God, which is your reasonable service. Romans 12:1

God is concerned about your body. That same body will someday get up from the grave and become a resurrected body that will go directly into the presence of God. There you will praise Him throughout all of eternity. Since your body will one day live with God in an eternal, miraculous, and incorruptible form, you need to get ready for that now. If you don't learn to praise Him down here, you'll never be able to praise Him throughout eternity.

THE INTERACTION OF BODY AND MIND

We humans are stimulated and motivated visually and experience much of life through our senses, but the interaction of body and mind is such that they stimulate and influence one another. There might be some legitimacy in saying that since God is a spirit and we are spirit beings, then our life with Him should operate only on the level of the spirit. Theoretically, we should be able to worship and commune with God with no physical involvement or physical manifestation at all. But the body-spirit-mind relationship is such that every mental or spiritual impulse carries with it a corresponding physical manifestation.

This physical manifestation, in some cases, is compulsive and inevitable. It cannot be suppressed, hidden, or avoided. Such reactions can be monitored with the use of the right equipment, and when they are, each physical impulse indicates the presence of a motivating thought or emotion. The greater and more intense the stimulus, the greater will be the physical manifestation. There are some things that happen on the inside that you cannot hide on the outside.

For instance, although not all of us turn red when we are embarrassed, if people watch us closely enough they can tell when we're embarrassed, upset, or otherwise impacted by something happening on the inside of us. What we think on the inside affects us on the outside. As we noted earlier in the book, Jeremiah decided that he would not say anything else about the Lord, but because he was thinking about the Lord, it didn't work:

Then I said, "I will not make mention of Him, nor speak anymore in His name." But His word was in my heart like a burning fire shut up in my bones; I was weary of holding it back, and I could not." Jeremiah 20:9

Jeremiah simply could not hold his peace. He had to say something. It was *"like a burning fire shut up in [his] bones."*

Soul rejoicing at its best becomes audible, physical sound. If you are rejoicing in God, you make noise. The psalmist David sang:

My soul shall make its boast in the Lord; the humble shall hear of it and be glad. Psalm 34:2-3

The soul boasts, but that boast is heard, and that makes others glad. What the soul does on the inside affects the outside, and others see and hear the results of it. Then, they, too, are *"glad."*

This phrase *"the humble"* is translated in the New Living Bible as *"all who are discouraged,"* and the rejoicing of your soul causes discouraged people to *"take heart."* Rejoice until some discouraged people take heart. Rejoice until some fallen people are lifted up. Rejoice until some wounded people are healed. When other people see your rejoicing, they will also begin to rejoice.

After David rejoiced in his soul, then he invited others to join him:

Oh, magnify the Lord with me, and let us exalt His name together. Psalm 34:3

They could not have exalted the name of the Lord *"together"* without making some noise, but that didn't bother David. He wasn't ashamed to worship God. He went much further in his worship. When he was blessed to bring the Ark of the Covenant back into Jerusalem after many years of exile, he became very physical indeed:

Then David danced before the Lord with all his might. 2 Samuel 6:14

At first, David was walking like everyone else. But then something hit a special note in his soul, and his body jumped in response. This brought more joy, and his feet began moving in a dance to God. In the process, his kingly cloak fell to the ground, but he didn't care. He went right on worshiping God in this beautiful way. He was grateful, he was happy, and he didn't care who knew it.

David's wife, the very proper daughter of King Saul, developed a terrible attitude about all of this. Was this the way a king should act in public? She thought not. But David could not be stopped. The Lord had lifted him up, his soul could not be stilled, and, therefore, his feet would not stop dancing.

In His Word, God has designated certain actions as acceptable expressions of our worship of Him, and no matter how sincere people are, they must abide by the instructions He has left us. The Tabernacle was given in its day as a visible and tangible instrument and symbol of praise and obedience to God, and if the people wanted to get to God, they had to deal with the thing, the place, or the custom just as God had ordered it. They were only symbols, but God had ordained them.

ORDAINED SYMBOLS

Even now, in the twenty-first century, God uses symbols. The Lord's Supper, for example, is symbolic. The bread we use is the symbol of our Lord's Body, and the fruit of the vine, or juice, is the symbol of His blood that was shed for our sins. In partaking of the bread and fruit of the vine, we reenact the drama of His death and suffering, and we are reminded of what He did for us on the cross.

Baptism is symbolic of the burial and resurrection of Christ and also of our burial with Him and our resurrection to salvation and eternal life. When we are baptized, we show others outwardly what has already happened to us inwardly.

The cross is an important symbol of our faith, and there are others. They all cause us to remember. The bread we use in communion is just bread, the cup is just juice, the water used in baptism is just water, and the crosses we use or wear are made of some common earthly material, but they all speak to us of our faith in Almighty God, and so they become vehicles by which we can enter into His very presence.

Symbols may be only reminders, but as such, they serve a very important purpose. One day, for instance, I was downstairs in my home, and I thought of something I needed upstairs. When I got upstairs, I couldn't remember what it was I had gone up to get. I stood there for a few minutes trying to think and decided that the only way I could remember what it was I needed was to go back downstairs where I had thought of it in the first place. And it worked.

That's what symbols do for us. They remind us. The bread, the communion cup, the waters of baptism, and the cross all help us to remember and to praise and worship the Lord.

As we begin now to take some specific steps into divine encounter in the Tabernacle, let us bear in mind the importance of holy places, holy objects, and holy acts. And may the journey lead us to discover the pathway to His presence.

Chapter   Three

THE BRAZEN ALTAR

SUBSTITUTION

You shall make an altar of acacia wood, five cubits long and five cubits wide—the altar shall be square—and its height shall be three cubits. ... And you shall overlay it with bronze. Exodus 27:1-2

Now this is what you shall offer on the altar: two lambs of the first year, day by day continually. One lamb you shall offer in the morning, and the other lamb you shall offer at twilight. With the one lamb shall be one-tenth of an ephah of flour mixed with one-fourth of a hin of pressed oil, and one-fourth of a hin of wine as a drink offering. And the other lamb you shall offer at twilight; and you shall offer with it the grain offering and the drink offering, as in the morning, for a sweet aroma, an offering made by fire to the Lord. This shall be a continual burnt offering throughout your generations at the door of the tabernacle of meeting before the Lord, where I will meet you to speak with you. And there I will meet with the children of Israel, and the tabernacle shall be sanctified by My glory. So I will consecrate the tabernacle of meeting and the altar. I will also consecrate both Aaron and his sons to minister to Me as priests. I will dwell among the children of Israel and will be their God. And they shall know that I am the Lord their God, who brought them up out of the land of Egypt, that I may dwell among them. I am the Lord their God. Exodus 29:38-46

If you are to have an encounter with God, you must understand what He intended at the Brazen Altar of the Tabernacle. This is your first stop, or your first step.

In the first chapter, we have seen that a relationship with God is everything. We must understand ourselves and our own motivation in such a relationship, and we must understand God's motive (He loves us), His objective (He wants to enjoy us and us to enjoy Him), His nature (He is holy and jealous, but merciful), and His promises (He will bountifully bless all those who sincerely seek to please Him). Having thus arrived at an adequate, practical, working understanding of God, we can better understand how to serve Him, what He is like, and what He expects from us.

There is, however, one factor that still hinders us. We need to explore more in depth what *we* are like and some of the factors that affect our ability (or our inability) to properly relate to God, to life, or, for that matter, to one another.

UNDERSTANDING MAN AND HIS NEED OF REDEMPTION

The Scriptures declare:

In the beginning God created the heavens and the earth. Genesis 1:1

The divine Word brought order out of chaos. The almighty and eternal God, in His wisdom, created and synchronized this vast universe in which we live. Upon the earth, He created various forms of plant and animal life. Then, as the finale to the great drama of Creation, God brought into existence a being made in His own image—man. This man (and the woman whom God gave to him) were esteemed and cherished above all that God had created. Man was a living soul who had the capacity to communicate with God, to love Him, and to worship Him.

The book of Genesis implies that in the world that God created there was not yet any death or physical suffering. The universe was a vast symphony of harmony and peace. Man was created in innocence and was privileged to live in communion and harmony with God and with all of creation.

God loved the man He had created, and because God loved man, He gave him a free will and made him a free moral being, with the ability to make choices regarding his moral and spiritual behavior. Although God had created man in purity and righteousness, Adam and Eve had to make their own choice as to whether or not they would maintain that purity and righteousness.

God had forbidden the man and the woman only one thing in all of creation, and this was important. The existence of alternatives is absolutely necessary if a person is to be a free moral being. Adam not only had to be free to do good; he also had to free to do evil. Otherwise he would not have been free at all.

The one thing that God prohibited for Adam and Eve was the fruit of the tree of the knowledge of good and evil, and He clearly informed them that the consequences of disobedience to Him in this regard would be death. It was man's desire to eat of this tree that would prove to be his downfall, and thus, sin would enter God's perfect world.

SIN ENTERED THE WORLD

The apostle John described sin as: *"the transgression of* [disobedience to] *the law* [the commands of God]" (1 John 3:4, KJV). Obedience to God, the Creator, was everything.

It was not long after God had placed Adam and Eve in their Eden before the tempter, Satan, presented himself to them. He said to the woman that God had lied about the tree of the knowledge of good and evil. "The fruit of that tree will make you like gods," he insisted. "It will not harm you; it will help you." (He continues to use this very same strategy today, and he doesn't even have any new lies. It's still the same old story: "It won't hurt you; God lied." Then he laughs at us as we move toward pain and destruction.)

Sin is the discordant note in the symphony of the universe.

The prospect of being gods was too much for Adam and Eve, and they disobeyed their Creator. We do not know the precise dynamics of the events and consequences that resulted from this disobedience. We cannot tell whether there was something about the essence of the fruit of the tree or some other causal factor involved in this fateful drama. But the undeniable fact is that Adam disobeyed God and that his disobedience had cosmic effects for the entire universe.

That instant of disobedience was the saddest and most tragic moment in all of human history. It would be impossible to chart the cosmic effects of sin. Sin is the discordant note in the symphony of the universe. It is the ugly blemish in God's picture of what the world ought to be. It is the disease that twisted man (who was made in the image of God) into a blasphemous satire of what God would have him to be.

Sin has emblazoned itself on the nature of the universe. It is a direct rebellion against almighty God. It is the deliberate transgression of His law. It is, as it were, a slap in the face of God. Therefore Adam's sin could not go unnoticed, and a curse came upon him.

SIN PASSED UPON ALL MEN

Adam's sinfulness had a legal and a hereditary effect upon all mankind. Adam stood as the legal representative of all men. When he, as the representative of men, disobeyed God and separated himself from Him, then all humanity was separated from God and was judged disobedient to the law of God. We are like an heir who inherits an already encumbered estate and proceeds to encumber it further with additional debt.

But not only do we have a legal relationship to Adam; we also have a hereditary relationship with him. Adam's nature was infected by sin, he became wicked and depraved, and he passed that sinfulness and depravity to every human being born on the face of the earth. Sin is a dread disease which is relayed from father and mother to son and daughter. All men are sinners, not only because Adam sinned, but also because they are sinners by nature, and every man has committed acts and emanated emotions that are an affront to the holiness and righteousness of God. As the Bible says, *"All have sinned, and come short of the glory of God,"* (Romans 3:23, KJV)—*"ALL."*

There are those who claim to believe that men are naturally good and righteous. They claim that if humans are left alone they will automatically do what is best and most virtuous. But there is little evidence in the annals of human history to substantiate this view. Rather, history has proven that man is exactly what the Bible says he is—a sinner.

In writing to the Romans, the apostle Paul described man and charged him with idolatry, sexual perversion, unrighteousness, vile affections, wickedness, fornication, covetousness, maliciousness, envy, murder, deceit, and opposition to God (see Romans 1). To these and many other sins, humanity must plead guilty.

Because of sinfulness and guilt, men became enemies of God and were made subject to the justice and the wrath of God. God's just nature demands that He reject sin and that He punish wickedness.

THE NECESSARY SUBSTITUTION

The condition of the world before the Fall is graphically portrayed in Genesis 1:29:

And God said, "See, I have given you every herb that yields seed which is on the face of all the earth, and every tree whose fruit yields seed; to you it shall be for food."

Man's diet apparently began as a vegetarian one, for the idea of killing and consuming the flesh of animals was not mentioned in the early part of Genesis. Even after man had sinned, the thought of killing animals did not seem to come to his mind:

Then the eyes of both of them were opened, and they knew that they were naked; and they sewed fig leaves together and made themselves coverings. Genesis 3:7

The King James Version of the Bible uses the term *"aprons"* to describe the covering Adam and Eve made for themselves. But any item of clothing made from leaves would have been very fragile and temporary. When they have dried, leaves easily disintegrate. And an *"apron"* would have been inadequate, because it only partially covered the body, not totally. God had a better idea:

Also for Adam and his wife the Lord God made tunics of skin, and clothed them. Genesis 3:21

The King James Version calls these tunics *"coats."* A coat more adequately covers the body, and one made of the skin of an animal would be much more durable than a garment of leaves. But in order for the skin of an animal to be obtained, that animal had to die; its blood must be shed. So from the time man sinned, bloodshed became necessary, so that man's guilt and shame might be covered.

In considering the need for a living sacrifice to atone for sin, we should take note of God's attitude toward the sacrifices offered by the son's of Adam and Eve:

And in process of time it came to pass, that Cain brought of the fruit of the ground an offering unto the Lord. And Abel, he also brought of the firstlings of his flock and of the fat thereof. And the Lord had respect unto Abel and to his offering. But unto Cain and to his offering he had not respect. Genesis 4:3-5, KJV

There is an implication here that a righteously indignant God found only the sacrifice and blood of a living animal to be acceptable as a substitute to make restitution for the sins of man. This is confirmed by the experience of the children of Israel in Egypt. When the death angel was sent to slay the firstborn of their slave masters (see Exodus 11), the Israelites were commanded to place the blood of a lamb on the lintel and doorposts of their homes. When the angel saw the blood, he would pass over them.

In the homes of those who were unprotected by the blood, every firstborn died that night. This, again, is the clear testimony of the Word of God that only the blood of a substitute can gain access for a sinful man into the presence of a righteous and holy God.

The writer of the book of Hebrews declared:

[In fact] under the Law almost everything is purified by means of blood, and without the shedding of blood there is neither release from sin and its guilt nor the remission of the due and merited punishment for sins. Hebrew 9:22, AMP

So then, it is categorical, not open to debate, and unavoidable that sin is such an abominable and repulsive phenomenon to our holy and righteous God that only an offering of blood can atone for it. In the Tabernacle, this was done at what was called the Brazen Altar.

WHAT WAS THE TABERNACLE ITSELF LIKE?

To understand the Brazen Altar, we must first step back and take a look at the Tabernacle itself. It was actually a relatively small tent-type structure, only forty-five feet long, fifteen feet wide, and about fifteen feet high. The walls of the Tabernacle were made of detachable boards that had been overlaid with gold. They were detachable because the Tabernacle had to be a portable structure that could be relatively easily disassembled and relocated as the Israelites moved from place to place on their way toward the Promised Land.

The ceiling of the Tabernacle was a curtain of purple, blue, and scarlet linen, with angels embroidered upon it. Over the linen ceiling was a covering of material made from goat's hair, and over that was a covering of rams' and goats' skins sewn together.

There was one door into the Tabernacle which entered a room called the Holy Place, and behind the Holy Place was another room, this one called the Most Holy Place, or Holy of Holies. This area was set apart by a veil made from the same material as the ceiling of the Tabernacle.

There was a fenced-in court, or yard, surrounding the Tabernacle called the Outer Court, or simply, the Court. It had a perimeter of four hundred and fifty feet. There was only one door into the Outer Court as well, and this one door lined up with the one door of the Tabernacle, both of them facing east.

The common people could enter only as far as the Outer Court. They could not go into the Holy Place, and they most certainly could not go into the Holy of Holies. The priests could go further than the common people, but only as far as the Holy Place. Only the High Priest (or Moses, in his day) could go into the Most Holy Place, and even the High Priest could go there only once a year—on the Day of Atonement.

THE FURNISHINGS OF THE TABERNACLE

The first item one would see upon entering the gate to the Outer Court was the Brazen Altar, or Altar of Sacrifice, as it was otherwise known. This altar was made of acacia wood, and then it was covered with bronze. It was seven and a half feet square and four and a half feet high.

Directly behind the Brazen Altar was the Laver, a basin where the priests had to wash themselves before performing any duties in the Court or in the Tabernacle. Inside the first room, the Holy Place, were the Table of Showbread, the Altar of Incense, and the Seven-Branched Candlestick. In the Most Holy Place, the Holy of Holies, behind the veil, was the awesome Ark of the Covenant where the presence of God dwelled, and, upon it, the Mercy Seat. Our focus, in this particular chapter, is the Brazen Altar.

The location of the Brazen Altar in the Tabernacle vividly informs us that the entrance into fellowship with God is by means of the Altar of Sacrifice. The individual worshipper, if he was not a priest, could go no further than this altar. (The priests, after first going to the Laver and the Brazen Altar, could go further as the representatives of the people.)

The Brazen Altar was a testimony of God's judgment and condemnation of sin. Every day two lambs were sacrificed on the altar—one in the morning and the other in the evening. Although the priests did the actual sacrificing, every Israelite who entered the Outer Court had to give half a shekel to support the service of the Tabernacle. With those funds, the lambs were purchased, so that every man or woman who came to the Brazen Altar was a participant, a stakeholder, and an investor in what took place there.

THE INNOCENT LAMB

The poor lamb had absolutely no choice in the matter. He most surely would not have willingly given his life for another. He was rudely snatched away from his mother, while she bleated and called for him. Afterward, she no doubt searched for him vainly for days, but her lamb could not be found. He had been sacrificed on the altar for the sins of mankind, sins that he had nothing to do with.

As the visitors to the Tabernacle watched the proceedings, seeing the blood of the poor lamb draining away, seeing the lamb being cut into pieces and burned on the altar, they would realize that this horrible death, butchery, and destruction by fire had all been made necessary by *their* sins and that this innocent lamb was dying in their place. These ceremonies created for the people of God a vivid awareness of the terrible effects of sin and the awful price required to atone for it. A lamb was dying because of the sins of a man.

It was not enough for the worshipper to merely participate in or observe this sacrifice; he was to identify with it, confessing his sins and repenting for them, and dedicating himself to the Lord anew in sincerity and devotion. At times, men laid their hands on the sacrifice, thus passing their sins to the innocent animal to be carried by them.

I can imagine what must have been going through the minds of those people:

> God, it should be me on that altar. I should have died because I have sinned. But You allowed me to offer this substitute. Thank You for giving me another chance. Now, since I have the privilege of continuing to live, although I surely don't deserve it, I must rededicate my life to You—everything that I am and everything that I have. You alone have made a way for my salvation. I love You, Lord.

As we have seen, the Bible declares that the Tabernacle and everything in it was a type, or shadow, of things to come. A shadow is merely a reflection of something else. What happened on the Brazen Altar confirmed that entrance into the things of God was available only through a sacrifice of blood and pointed to a better sacrifice to come:

> *And every priest stands ministering daily and offering repeatedly the same sacrifices, which can never take away sins. But this Man, after He had offered one sacrifice for sins forever, sat down at the right hand of God, from that time waiting till His enemies are made His footstool. For by one offering He has perfected forever those who are being sanctified.* Hebrews 10:11-14

The sacrificial lambs of the Tabernacle were merely a type of Christ, and God accepted them during that time only because they signaled what was to come for all mankind. Jesus, the Son of God, would come to the earth wrapped in mortal flesh and would die for the sins of the whole world.

A VERY SPECIAL SUBSTITUTE

We needed a very special sacrifice to atone for our sins. First of all, we needed a substitute who was innocent. If the substitute was not innocent, then he would have had to suffer for his own sins and not ours. Lambs were an acceptable substitute in their time because they *could* not sin. It was impossible for them to do so. Therefore God ordained that lambs would suffer in the place of men.

> *Jesus was the perfect substitute because He was innocent, sinless.*

But animals were far from perfect substitutes because they were not directly related to man. It was man who had sinned, not lambs, so a perfect sacrifice would have to be a man. We needed a substitute who was related to us.

We also needed a substitute who was all-encompassing. This would not be the death of one man for another; it would be the death of one man for all men who had lived in the past, all men who were currently living, and all men who would ever live in the future. An exhaustive search was conducted throughout all of creation, and only one was found who was worthy. His name was Jesus.

Jesus was the perfect substitute because He was innocent, sinless:

For He made Him who knew no sin to be sin for us, that we might become the righteousness of God in Him. 2 Corinthians 5:21

[He] was in all points tempted like as we are, yet without sin. Hebrews 4:15

Jesus was the perfect substitute because He was related to us. Although He was God, He was also fully man, born in the flesh, *"born of a woman"*:

But when the fullness of the time had come, God sent forth His Son, born of a woman, born under the law, to redeem those who were under the law, that we might receive the adoption as sons. Galatians 4:4-5

Jesus was the perfect substitute because He was worthy. After all, He was fully God:

And the Word became flesh and dwelt among us, and we beheld His glory, the glory as of the only begotten of the Father, full of grace and truth. John 1:14

John saw the Lamb in heaven, where His worthiness was recognized and lauded:

Then I saw a strong angel proclaiming with a loud voice, "Who is worthy to open the scroll and to loose its seals?" And no one in heaven or on the earth or under the earth was able to open the scroll, or to look at it. So I wept much, because no one was found worthy to open and read the scroll, or to look at it.

But one of the elders said to me, "Do not weep. Behold, the Lion of the tribe of Judah, the Root of David, has prevailed to open the scroll and to loose its seven seals."

And I looked, and behold, in the midst of the throne and of the four living creatures, and in the midst of the elders, stood a Lamb as though it had been slain, having seven horns and seven eyes, which are the seven Spirits of God sent out into all the earth. Then He came and took the scroll out of the right hand of Him who sat on the throne. Revelation 5:2-7

It was then that the four living creatures and the twenty-four elders fell down before Him and worshiped and sang a new song, one that proclaimed His worthiness:

"You are worthy to take the scroll, and to open its seals; for You were slain, and have redeemed us to God by Your blood out of every tribe and tongue and people and nation, and have made us kings and priests to our God; and we shall reign on the earth." Revelation 5:9-10

Then the angels joined the chorus. They, too, recognized His worthiness:

"Worthy is the Lamb who was slain to receive power and riches and wisdom, and strength and honor and glory and blessing!" Revelation 5:12

Yes, our Lord was worthy.

So Jesus met all of the conditions. He was innocent; He was related to us; and He was more than worthy. Thus He became our eternal substitute, the lamb upon the Brazen Altar, *"slain from the foundation of the world"* (Revelation 13:8). The cross became His Brazen Altar, and He was nailed to it. As the great songwriter Isaac Watts (1674-1748) declared in 1707:

> *At the cross, at the cross where I first saw the light*
> *And the burden of my heart rolled away.*
> *It was there by faith I received my sight.*
> *And now I am happy all the day.*

Nails pierced His hands and feet, and a crown of thorns was pressed down upon His skull. It was not something that He, as a man, wanted to have happen. He had prayed for this burden to be removed from Him, but in the end He willingly went to the cross.

The little lamb in the Tabernacle had no say about his fate of being hung upon the Brazen Altar for the sins of men, but Jesus could easily have refused. It was His great love for us that caused Him not to. He prayed, *"Not as I will,"* (Matthew 26:39, KJV), *"Thy will be done"* (verse 42).

Rather than think of His own comfort and physical well-being, Jesus chose to act for the good of all mankind, for the survival of the human race, for the eternal salvation of men everywhere. Thus declares the Word of God:

Greater love has no one than this, than to lay down one's life for his friends. John 15:13

It was for us, as Isaiah shows us:

He was wounded for our transgressions, He was bruised for our iniquities; the chastisement for our peace was upon Him, and by His stripes we are healed. All we like sheep have gone astray; We have turned, every one, to his own way; and the Lord has laid on Him the iniquity of us all. Isaiah 53:5-6

GO TO THE CROSS TODAY

The priests of the Old Testament Tabernacle had to go by the Brazen Altar every day on their way to the Holy Place, and every day we ought to go by way of the cross. We don't have to visit a church to do it; we can do it anywhere.

We should go to the cross to repent sincerely. We should go there to seek God's help. We should go there to seek and claim forgiveness. We should go there to rededicate ourselves to the work of God. After all, since we live *because* of Him, we should live *for* Him.

You may have been saved for many years, but you still need to visit the cross. You may not have any sins of commission, but you have surely committed sins of omission. We all have.

Did you speak to everyone you met today about Christ? Did you do every good you could have done today? Did you lift up the fallen around you today? No matter how holy you think you are, you must bow before the cross every day, recognizing that it is a sin to come short of the mark. *"All our righteousnesses are as filthy rags"* before Him (Isaiah 64:6). God is so high above us that there is no way we could reach His holiness and righteousness. So bow your knee at the cross and recognize it. Ask God to forgive you and to let you experience Calvary afresh and anew.

It was your sins that nailed Jesus to the cross, and if you now feel that you can live without His help, you are crucifying Him afresh. Plus, you are in for a rude awakening. You will be miserably disappointed, because you simply cannot make it on your own. Jesus said:

Without me ye can do nothing. John 15:5, KJV

He went on to say that the opposite is also true:

If ye abide in me, and my words abide in you, ye shall ask what ye will, and it shall be done unto you. John 15:7, KJV

Because Christ is the Source of our strength as Christians, every day we should focus our hearts and minds on *Him* and on what *He* has done for us on Calvary. The songwriter John Bowring (1792-1872) declared in 1825, "In the cross of Christ I glory," and Paul, the apostle, agreed:

God forbid that I should glory, save in the cross of our Lord Jesus Christ. Galatians 6:14, KJV

The cross is the place where God makes provision so that He can meet with otherwise tainted men and women. Don't fail to take advantage of what He has done there. It doesn't matter what you have done; there is forgiveness for it at the cross. As the songwriter Charlotte Elliott (1789-1871) declared in 1835:

Just as I am, without one plea,
But that Thy blood was shed for me.
And that thou bidst me come to Thee,
Oh, Lamb of God, I come.

The sacrifice of the blood of Jesus on the cross is adequate to atone for all of our sins. There exists no sin that He is powerless to cleanse. As the songwriters, Fanny Crosby (1820-1915) and Robert Lowry (1826-1899) wrote in 1875 in their hymn "To God Be the Glory":

The vilest offender who truly believes
That moment from Jesus a pardon receives.

We are so self-centered these days, and we want our religion to be convenient.

"That moment": do it today, and do it without delay.

WHAT CAN WE SACRIFICE FOR HIM?

When I think about the nails in His hands and feet, about the crown of thorns upon His head, about Him hanging there from the sixth hour until the ninth hour with blood streaming steadily down his body, and without having a free hand to wipe the flies away from His face, when I think of Him naked before the taunts of men, and I realize that it was all for me, something deep inside of me begins to respond. I ask, "What can I do for the Lord? What can I give Him? What can I sacrifice for His glory?"

We are so self-centered these days, and we want our religion to be convenient. We don't want to go out of our way for anything or anybody. We don't want to sacrifice at all. But I hear Jesus saying, "I gave My life for you, and if I could give My life for you, at the very least you should be willing to *live* for Me." So, I'll live for Him who died for me. I'll live for Him who shed His blood that I might have life and life more abundantly. I'll live for Him who atoned on my behalf, to pick me up, turn me around, and set my life on a very different course.

How about you? Have you made up your mind to live for Him?

STAY UNDER THE BLOOD

Are you under the blood of Jesus today? When the first Passover came, the Israelites had to stay at home as the death angel passed over them. If they had left the safety of their homes, they would have been outside the covering of the blood, and they would have been destroyed. So they stayed put inside the homes where the blood had been applied.

Child of God, don't be so quick to go your own way. Stay under the blood of Jesus. Let your faith always be in His sacrifice, and always let your plea be the blood of Jesus. As long as you stay under the blood, the devil cannot approach you.

He fears the blood and cannot come where it is applied. He is repelled by it and quickly driven away. Stay under the blood because your salvation is in the blood. Stay under the blood because your healing is in the blood. Stay under the blood because when you're under the blood, you can stand before God Himself just as if you had never committed a single sin. Paul wrote:

> *There is therefore now no condemnation to those who are in Christ Jesus, who do not walk according to the flesh, but according to the Spirit. For the law of the Spirit of life in Christ Jesus has made me free from the law of sin and death.* Romans 8:1-2

DON'T WAIT

Go to the cross today. Don't wait.

We should not only go to the cross for repentance and forgiveness, but also to give thanks. We have so much to praise God for. He has been so good to each of us. He has opened doors that we cannot see and made ways when no ways previously existed. He held onto us when others would have cast us aside. Of the many things He has done for us, the most important is to make the provision of the sacrifice for our sins. That is what gives us access to the rest of God's blessings.

I can assure you that if you had been the only sinner on the face of the whole earth, Jesus would have died for you—because He loves you so much. Rest in that assurance today, receive His forgiveness, and rejoice in it.

The Israelites who frequented the wilderness Tabernacle could not help but rejoice because they had there before them on the altar a physical reminder of what they deserved. "That could have been me," they had to be thinking. "And because it's not me, I want to give God thanks and praise."

Every day, as I walk down the street and see homeless people pushing their meager belongings around in an old worn-out shopping cart, I have to give God thanks. I know that it could have been me. I could have been homeless, with no food to eat and no clothes to wear. I could have been just another number, a nameless face on the streets of some modern American city. God has been so good to me.

JUST THE FIRST STEP

Before concluding this chapter, we should note again that the Brazen Altar is just the first stop, or the first step. From there, we must decide that we will go all the way to the Mercy Seat. In the time of the wilderness Tabernacle, all the people could do was return to this altar over and over again. They had no more left the grounds of the Tabernacle than they must have felt the need to reenter it again. Their only recourse was endless sacrifices upon the Brazen Altar, for that was as far as they could go. But when Jesus hung on the cross for our sins, He opened up a new and a living way, allowing us to go right on into the Holy Place and even into the Holy of Holies—right to the very the Mercy Seat.

When it happened, suddenly the veil of the Temple in Jerusalem was mysteriously and miraculously ripped in two. This tearing began at the top and continued to the bottom. Suddenly, the Most Holy Place was exposed to everyone. A way had been opened into God's presence for all men.

No one could doubt it, and no one could doubt that God had done it. That let us know, as Hebrews says:

Seeing then that we have a great high priest, that is passed into the heavens, Jesus the Son of God, let us hold fast our profession. For we have not an high priest which cannot be touched with the feeling of our infirmities; but was in all points tempted like as we are, yet without sin. Let us therefore come boldly unto the throne of grace, that we may obtain mercy, and find grace to help in time of need. Hebrews 4:14-16

We need not come to our holy and righteous and jealous God timidly or reluctantly. We may now come boldly, Jesus having prepared for us the way.

Once at His throne, we may *"obtain mercy, and find grace."* The mercy will help us with sins already committed, and the grace will help us with weaknesses that may characterize us and with challenges that may stand before us.

Child of God, you can *"obtain mercy"* and *"find grace to help"* you in your time of need. As John Newton (1725-1807) wrote in 1779:

Through many dangers, toils, and snares I have already come.
'Twas grace that brought me safe thus far, and grace will see me home.

There is much blessing yet to come, and more giant steps to take into God's very presence. Are you ready to pass beyond the Outer Court? Personally I want to go everywhere the grace of God can take me. I'm not satisfied just to step inside the door. I want to go all the way. I want to participate with the saints of God everywhere in what it means to advance into the very throne room of God and to commune with Him as never before.

I don't want any more veils separating me from the things He has prepared for me. Every day I want to get closer to Him. Every day I want to know Him more. Every day I want to go higher. Every day I want a greater anointing. No more dillydallying around in the shallows for me! I'm ready to plunge into the deepest parts of the grace of God.

Why should I stay around the door any longer? I am determined to go through the Outer Court, then through the Holy Place and right on beyond the veil into the Holy of Holies—to the very presence of Almighty God. I hope that is your determination as well. Prepare your-self to advance and to do it quickly. You're getting closer to your divine encounter.

Chapter Four

THE BRONZE LAVER
CLEANSING

Then the Lord spoke to Moses, saying: "You shall also make a laver of bronze, with its base also of bronze, for washing. You shall put it between the tabernacle of meeting and the altar. And you shall put water in it, for Aaron and his sons shall wash their hands and their feet in water from it. When they go into the tabernacle of meeting, or when they come near the altar to minister, to burn an offering made by fire to the Lord, they shall wash with water, lest they die. So they shall wash their hands and their feet, lest they die. And it shall be a statute forever to them—to him and his descendants throughout their generations." Exodus 30:17-21

He made the laver of bronze and its base of bronze, from the bronze mirrors of the serving women who assembled at the door of the tabernacle of meeting. Exodus 38:8

He set the laver between the tabernacle of meeting and the altar, and put water there for washing; and Moses, Aaron, and his sons would wash their hands and their feet with water from it. Whenever they went into the tabernacle of meeting, and when they came near the altar, they washed, as the Lord had commanded Moses. Exodus 40:30-32

The Laver symbolized moral and spiritual purification and cleansing.

If you are to have an encounter with God, you must come by way of the Bronze Laver.

We started this journey in an attempt to reach the Ark of the Covenant, but we quickly learned that in order to reach it, we had to pass by the Brazen Altar and the Bronze Laver, we had to go into the Holy Place, by the Lampstand, the Table of Showbread and the Golden Altar of Incense and still the Veil prevented us from entering the Holy of Holies where the Ark was kept. Only after passing through that veil could we reach the coveted prize, the place where God's presence dwelled. Some people just want to burst into God's presence without passing anything, but clearly there is a process we must go through to reach that level. Let us now take another step.

WHAT WAS THE LAVER?

The Bronze Laver was the second item that one would see after entering the Court of the Tabernacle. It was situated between the door of the Outer Court and the Brazen Altar. But what exactly was it? This word *laver* merely means "a basin or bowl." God directed that this very special bowl be made of brass and that it was to be kept filled with water.

The brass with which the Laver was made was a very shiny and reflective brass, because it was actually made from brass mirrors that the women of Israel contributed. Later, we will seek some significance in this fact.

The Laver had a base that supported it and was designed in such a way that the priests could wash both hands and feet from the water within it. This water was frequently changed, so that it would remove contamination and filth rather than adding to it.

The Laver symbolized moral and spiritual purification and cleansing. While the Brazen Altar symbolized release from the guilt, the penalty, and the condemnation of sin, the Laver focused on the individual priest seeking to distance himself from the contamination of sin. It stressed the determination of the worshipper to renounce and reject sinful behavior and to come before the Lord without the stain of immoral acts or thoughts. Thus, the Laver was an expression of respect for the holy nature of God.

It should be noted again that only the priests approached the Laver. The ordinary worshipper could only come in the gate and stand before the Brazen Altar. Only the priests could go to the Laver and then on into the Holy Place. And, again, only the High Priest could go into the Most Holy Place, or the Holy of Holies. But it should also be noted, again, that in that day whatever the priests did, they did as the representatives of the people. They were the agents and ambassadors of the people. God had chosen them and set them aside as holy unto Himself so that they could commune with Him on behalf of His people.

We should not resent this system or feel that the people were deprived, because the priests bore a hosts of restrictions and responsibilities from which the common people were relieved. Jesus taught:

For everyone to whom much is given, from him much will be required; and to whom much has been committed, of him they will ask the more. Luke 12:48

Also, we should realize that Jesus functioned as our High Priest when He carried on His redemptive and atoning work. Most of all, *we* should relate to the priests because the Bible indicates that under the New Covenant economy we are priests of God:

To Him who loved us and washed us from our sins in His own blood, and has made us kings and priests to His God and Father, to Him be glory and dominion forever and ever. Revelation 1:5-6

So in essence many of the things that the priests or the High Priest did and experienced are symbolic of what we, as priests of God, must do and experience. Therefore we must study these men in their dispensation to better understand our role as priests unto God in our own dispensation. And one of the things they did frequently was to wash in the Bronze Laver.

RECOGNIZING THE NEED FOR CLEANSING

As we have noted, the Brazen Altar was the first item that one would see upon entering the court of the congregation and the Laver was the second, but although the priests would *see* the Brazen Altar first, it was to the Laver that they would *go* first. There they must first be cleansed.

When any man became a priest, Moses, as a part of the priestly consecration, was directed to wash them completely at the Laver. They had to respect God enough to allow themselves to be prepared to stand before Him.

Even Moses was taught to honor God. As we have seen, when he approached God at the burning bush, God said to him, "Wait! Before you come closer, honor and respect Me by taking off your shoes. Prepare yourself to come into My presence." This implies that in genuine conversion and in sincere worship there should be a prior sense and recognition of uncleanness and unworthiness and an internal and external manifestation of repentance, a renunciation of that which has offended God. There should also be a desire to be free of it.

We don't just force ourselves into the presence of God. We must first recognize our unworthiness to even be there in the first place, and then we must seek His cleansing. We somehow have to recognize that it is only by the grace of God through Jesus that we have the privilege of entering that holy place, and before we attempt it, there should first be repentance and renunciation of sin.

Most of us have been wronged by someone who, the next time they saw us, walked right up to us as if nothing had occurred. We know how very offensive this can be. We didn't even want to talk to them until some unfinished business was taken care of.

There is also a proper way to enter the Lord's presence:

Enter into His gates with thanksgiving, and into His courts with praise. Be thankful to Him, and bless His name. Psalm 100:4

Don't wait until you get to the Brazen Altar or the Laver to start praying and worshiping; begin at the door. Some people are all foolishness, and then suddenly they become serious when they want something from God. But that's not the way to receive from Him.

A tradition of former times was for the saints to go directly to the altar or prayer room when they had arrived at their church and there to pray and seek God before they had done anything else. Today we spend our time greeting one another. But God is number one, and we should greet Him properly before greeting anyone else. Get your spirit right and get in tune with God before you do anything else so that you can then receive something from Him.

John the Baptist said it this way:

Therefore bear fruits worthy of repentance. Matthew 3:8

When you come before God, get the order of business right. First go by the Laver and pray, "Lord, I know that I'm not what I should be. Clean me up. Purify my soul. I want to be pleasing in Your sight."

Paul wrote to the Corinthian church:

For godly sorrow produces repentance leading to salvation, not to be regretted; but the sorrow of the world produces death. 2 Corinthians 7:10

Trying to face God without sincerely repenting is an affront to His holiness. Admit your guilt before Him and seek His forgiveness.

Luke recorded the story of a rich tax collector who had an encounter with Jesus:

Then Jesus entered and passed through Jericho. Now behold, there was a man named Zacchaeus who was a chief tax collector, and he was rich. And he sought to see who Jesus was, but could not because of the crowd, for he was of short stature. So he ran ahead and climbed up into a sycamore tree to see Him, for He was going to pass that way. And when Jesus came to the place, He looked up and saw him, and said to him, "Zacchaeus, make haste and come down, for today I must stay at your house."

So he made haste and came down, and received Him joyfully. But when they saw it, they all complained, saying, "He has gone to be a guest with a man who is a sinner."

Then Zacchaeus stood and said to the Lord, "Look, Lord, I give half of my goods to the poor; and if I have taken anything from anyone by false accusation, I restore fourfold."

And Jesus said to him, "Today salvation has come to this house, because he also is a son of Abraham; for the Son of Man has come to seek and to save that which was lost." Luke 19:1-10

The people of that day looked down on Zacchaeus as a terrible sinner, and I suppose he was. But he had a hunger in his heart to see Jesus. Being a short man, he climbed up in a tree so that he could catch a glimpse of the Master as He went by. How badly do you want to see Him?

With his ill-gotten wealth, Zacchaeus had reached new levels of society. He was now part of the upper crust, but he was not too high-falluting that day to climb a tree to see the Lord, and that fact caught the Lord's attention.

Jesus looked up at Zacchaeus and knew immediately what was in the man's heart. He also knew that He would lodge at Zacchaeus' house that evening.

Notice the reaction of the little man to this invitation: *"So he made haste and came down, and received Him joyfully."* Zacchaeus did not consider the Lord's visit to his house an imposition, but rather a privilege, and he *"received Him joyfully."* Then, overwhelmed by the fact that Jesus would honor him in this way, by actually staying at his house, Zacchaeus immediately began to confess his wrong and to think of ways to make amends for it. That's the response the Lord is looking for from us as well.

The people standing around that day were offended that Jesus would spend the evening with such a notorious sinner as Zacchaeus, but Jesus said that salvation had come to the house of Zacchaeus. Just being in the presence of Jesus brought such guilt and condemnation to Zacchaeus' soul that he wanted to be clean, and he was ready to do whatever was necessary to atone for the past. If you can just look into the eyes of Jesus, your life will be changed too.

THE TRUE REFLECTION OF ONESELF

Since the Laver was made from the bronze mirrors donated by the women who stood outside the gate of the Tabernacle, it is not inconceivable that one coming to the Laver might be able to see his own reflection as he looked at it. This would enable him to see himself in all of his unworthiness. That reflection, compared with the holiness of God, would cause worshippers to say, "I must wash. I must be cleansed." This is what happened to Zacchaeus as he looked upon Jesus. He could see his own unworthiness and knew that cleansing was needed.

Isaiah went to the house of the Lord, and he was similarly impacted. No sooner had Isaiah seen the holiness of God than he recognized how impure he himself was. *"Woe is me!"* he cried (Isaiah 6:5), and because there was a recognition of unworthiness, there was also a remedy. An angel immediately flew to the altar, got a hot coal from it, and came back to Isaiah. Then, with one touch, the prophet was cleansed. His *"iniquity"* was *"taken away,"* and his *"sin"* was *"purged"* (verse 7).

Anytime we are reminded of what a holy God we serve, it becomes apparent that we need to be prepared ourselves to enter into His presence.

YOU CANNOT CLEANSE YOURSELF

It was Moses who first washed Aaron and his sons. Only later would they be allowed to wash themselves:

> *And Aaron and his sons you shall bring to the door of the tabernacle of meeting, and you shall wash them with water.* Exodus 29:4

This initial washing was symbolic of the initial washing of regeneration done by Jesus Christ through the Holy Spirit. If we are to be cleansed, Jesus will have to do it by the application of His righteousness.

This was not something the priests could have done for themselves; it had to be done by Moses, who was a type of Jesus. Even the Laver itself was a type of Christ:

> *Not by works of righteousness which we have done, but according to His mercy He saved us, through the washing of regeneration and renewing of the Holy Spirit, whom He poured out on us abundantly through Jesus Christ our Savior.* Titus 3:5-6

When Jesus comes into your life, He breaks the rule of the old man of sin, canceling his authority, and He brings into existence a new man who is to take charge of your life through the power of the Holy Spirit. Paul wrote:

> *Christ also loved the church and gave Himself for her, that He might sanctify and cleanse her with the washing of water by the word, that He might present her to Himself a glorious church, not*

having spot or wrinkle or any such thing, but that she should be holy and without blemish. Ephesians 5:25-27

We come to God just as we are, tainted by sin, and He thoroughly washes us. If you will surrender to Him today, He will give you a good Holy Ghost scrub-down right now.

THE NEED FOR A NEW LIFE

Jesus called for a new life in each of us:

Jesus answered and said to him, "Most assuredly, I say to you, unless one is born again, he cannot see the kingdom of God."

Nicodemus said to Him, "How can a man be born when he is old? Can he enter a second time into his mother's womb and be born?"

Jesus answered, "Most assuredly, I say to you, unless one is born of water and the Spirit, he cannot enter the kingdom of God. That which is born of the flesh is flesh, and that which is born of the Spirit is spirit. Do not marvel that I said to you, 'You must be born again.' " John 3:3-7

Paul wrote of a freedom from the *"condemnation"* of sin and a new life in Christ:

There is therefore now no condemnation to those who are in Christ Jesus, who do not walk according to the flesh, but according to the Spirit. Romans 8:1

Therefore, if anyone is in Christ, he is a new creation; old things have passed away; behold, all things have become new. 2 Corinthians 5:17

These scriptures indicate that when a person accepts Jesus Christ, a righteous nature and capacity comes into existence within him [or her]. You cannot live in the Spirit until you have been born of the Spirit. Why are so many trying to live a righteous life without first having truly accepted Jesus or believed on the sacrifice of His blood? If He is not our Lord and Savior, there is no way we can live righteously in this world.

When we do come to Him, He washes us:

Do you not know that the unrighteous will not inherit the kingdom of God? Do not be deceived. Neither fornicators, nor idolaters, nor adulterers, nor homosexuals, nor sodomites, nor thieves, nor covetous, nor drunkards, nor revilers, nor extortioners will inherit the kingdom of God. And such were some of you. But you were washed, but you were sanctified, but you were justified in the name of the Lord Jesus and by the Spirit of our God. 1 Corinthians 6:9-11

> *We are both forgiven and given new life by the Spirit of God in the same moment.*

For the priests of the Old Testament, the initial washing at the Laver took place before they went to the Brazen Altar for atonement. But for the believer in Christ Jesus, atonement and regeneration take place at the same time. We are both forgiven and given new life by the Spirit of God in the same moment. Forgiveness and the born-again experience come in one package.

When Jesus died on the cross, a soldier pierced Him in the side, and the Bible says, *"immediately blood and water came out"* (John 19:34). This indicated that, in Christ, the blood of absolution, the blood for removal of guilt, would be forever mixed with the water of cleansing.

CLEANSING MUST BE CONTINUAL

But let us remember that the priest not only went to the Laver when they were first consecrated; they went there again and again as they performed their priestly duties. Each time they went outside the tabernacle court and returned they would wash their hands and feet at the Laver.

As they moved around in the Tabernacle their feet would get dirty because there was no covering on the floor; it was just bare ground. So they would go frequently to the Laver. As they handled the sacrifices and tended the fire upon the Brazen Altar, their hands would get dirty, and they would go again to the Laver. Before they could go into the Holy Place (and before the High Priest could go into the Most Holy Place), they had to be clean. So they would go to the Laver and wash.

This frequent washing of their hands indicated sorrow and repentance for sin, the renunciation of sin, the cleansing of their minds, of their hearts, and of their spirits before Almighty God.

The psalmist declared:

Who may ascend into the hill of the Lord? Or who may stand in His holy place? He who has clean hands and a pure heart, who has not lifted up his soul to an idol, nor sworn deceitfully. He shall receive blessing from the Lord, and righteousness from the God of his salvation. Psalm 24:3-5

We are forgiven and sanctified as soon as we are saved. When the Lord comes into our hearts, He cleanses us and sets us apart for Himself. But it is sometimes difficult to stay clean after we have been washed. Why try to hide that fact?

Our bodies, our clothing, our houses, and our automobiles get dirty just because they are here on this earth. You don't have to be doing anything wrong to get dirty here. This earth is a dirty place and earthly "stuff" settles on everything. Just sit here, and in time you will be dirty. No matter how careful you are with your appearance, somebody can drive by, hit a mud puddle, and mess you up in a moment.

Spiritually and morally, our situation is the same. This body of flesh, and these fleshly, selfish, pleasure-focused minds of ours are always proposing some kind of wrong and evil involvement. Even if you don't do wrong, you can feel dirty after listening to your mind talk all day.

But we do sin. The devil and sinful people try to bring the dirt of sin into our lives, and sometimes they succeed. Sometimes Christians are carried away by a wave of evil passion that sweeps over them, and they suddenly find themselves soiled.

There are other ways to become unclean. The stress and strain of life has a way of pulling the good out of you and replacing it with bitterness and anger, and folks can hurt you and mistreat you, causing you to want to do the same to them. Sometimes we become dirty, not because of something we have done, but because of our response to something someone else has done to us. Also, habits that you thought you had long ago escaped have a way of showing up again during a time of vulnerability. Still, we are commanded to be holy in this world.

WHAT, THEN, IS THE MESSAGE?

So the message to the New Testament believer is: (1) Understand that you have been washed, and if God washed you, it's because He wants you clean. If He had wanted you dirty, He would not have washed you in the first place. So don't jump into every mud puddle you pass. You've been washed. Make every effort to stay clean:

> For if, after they have escaped the pollutions of the world through the knowledge of the Lord and Savior Jesus Christ, they are again entangled in them and overcome, the latter end is worse for them than the beginning. For it would have been better for them not to have known the way of righteousness, than having known it, to turn from the holy commandment delivered to them. But it has happened to them according to the true proverb: "A dog returns to his own vomit," and, "a sow, having washed, to her wallowing in the mire."
> 2 Peter 2:20-22

When God pulls you out of the muck and mire and cleanses you, it is not His will for you to jump right back into the same stuff.

The message is: (2) If you fall down, don't just lie there; get up and move on:

If we confess our sins, He is faithful and just to forgive us our sins and to cleanse us from all unrighteousness. 1 John 1:9

Child of God, you can get back up. God has also promised to *"keep you from falling"*:

Now to Him who is able to keep you from stumbling [falling, KJV], *and to present you faultless before the presence of His glory with exceeding joy...* Jude 24

Our God *"is able to keep you from falling,"* so get up and go on. He is able *"to present you faultless before the presence of His glory,"* so get up and go on.

The message is: (3) Remember the importance of your spirit and your soul. Your body will return to dust, but your spirit will live on forever:

And do not fear those who kill the body but cannot kill the soul. But rather fear Him who is able to destroy both soul and body in hell. Matthew 10:28

Your body (your flesh) tells you many things, but you need to have a little talk with it and remind it that it is just here for a few years, but you're here for eternity. It will return to the dust, decay, and become rotten, but you will live on forever somewhere and will have to stand before God and give an account of the deeds done in the flesh:

So then each of us shall give account of himself to God. Romans 14:12

And there is no creature hidden from His sight, but all things are naked and open to the eyes of Him to whom we must give account. Hebrews 4:13

Tell your flesh that you refuse to let it ruin your chances at eternity. Say, "Flesh, we are going to live for God and walk in His ways," and then enforce that determination.

The message is: (4) Remember who you are and whose you are:

Peter wrote:

But you are a chosen generation, a royal priesthood, a holy nation, His own special people, that you may proclaim the praises of Him who called you out of darkness into His marvelous light. 1 Peter 2:9

I'm a child of the King, and I'm a priest of the most high God, so I can't walk like others walk, and I can't live like others live. I also can't dress like others dress. My life has to be different, because I must be pleasing in the eyes of Almighty God.

The message is: (5) Remember the promises God has made to you:

Never forget those promises made to Israel (and subsequently to you), that you would be the head and not the tail (meaning that you would be on the top, not the bottom), that you would lend and not borrow, that all nations would rise up and call you blessed. Paul wrote:

Therefore, having these promises, beloved, let us cleanse ourselves from all filthiness of the flesh and spirit, perfecting holiness in the fear of God. 2 Corinthians 7:1

Child of God, when I think of the agenda God has in mind for me, it makes me want to get on the path that leads to my blessing, the path that leads to my prosperity.

The message is: (6) If you can get close to God, He will lead you and guide you. If you can get close to Him, His holiness and righteousness will rub off on you:

Draw near to God and He will draw near to you. Cleanse your hands, you sinners; and purify your hearts, you double-minded. Lament and mourn and weep! Let your laughter be turned to mourning and your joy to gloom. Humble yourselves in the sight of the Lord, and He will lift you up. James 4:8-10

Jesus said:

You are already clean because of the word which I have spoken to you. Abide in Me, and I in you. As the branch cannot bear fruit of itself, unless it abides in the vine, neither can you, unless you abide in Me. John 15:3-4

The message is: (7) If you want to be clean, focus your mind on clean things, on holy things, on good things:

The apostle Paul wrote to the Philippian believers:

> *Finally, brethren, whatever things are true, whatever things are noble, whatever things are just, whatever things are pure, whatever things are lovely, whatever things are of good report, if there is any virtue and if there is anything praiseworthy—meditate on these things. The things which you learned and received and heard and saw in me, these do, and the God of peace will be with you.* Philippians 4:8-9

If you want to be clean, focus your mind on clean things, on holy things, on good things

"Meditate on these things." Tell others, including your own flesh, that you refuse to think about what they want you to think about. Focus your mind on God, and meditate on His Word:

> *How can a young man cleanse his way? By taking heed according to Your word. With my whole heart I have sought You; oh, let me not wander from Your commandments! Your word I have hidden in my heart, that I might not sin against You.* Psalm 119:9-11

God's Word hidden in your heart will keep you from sinning against Him. When you have His Word hidden on the inside, it will be *"a lamp to [your] feet, ... a light to [your] path"* (Psalm 119:105).

The message is: (8) Be baptized in and filled with the Holy Spirit and get the power of God working in your life:

But you shall receive power when the Holy Spirit has come upon you; and you shall be witnesses to Me in Jerusalem, and in all Judea and Samaria, and to the end of the earth. Acts 1:8

But you, beloved, building yourselves up on your most holy faith, praying in the Holy Spirit... Jude 20

I'm sure that your intentions are good, but you need the power of God to help you do what you mean to do, to help you do what you know is right to do, to help you to keep your resolve and keep your commitments to God. There is nothing quite like having Holy Ghost power on the inside of you. It is power to do the will of God, power to walk in His ways.

He is *"able to keep you from falling."* You're not able, but He is. You can't make it, but He can make it for you. You can't do it, but Christ in you is *"the hope of glory"* (Colossians 1:27). You can't stand, but He can stand inside of you. And when you stumble, He will keep you from falling. Your strength will run out, but then His strength will step in and take over. And when you're about to fall, He'll put you back on your feet.

DROP ALL YOUR PRETENSIONS

Have you ever gone to a restaurant to have a nice meal, and you picked up a fork or knife and was about to use it, or a cup and were about to drink from it, when you noticed that it was dirty? Most of us have had this experience, and our response is almost always the same. We call the waiter or waitress and ask them to take it back and wash it again. We want a clean one.

Far too many people present themselves arrogantly before God, and when He holds them up to the light, He notices that they have not been cleansed. "Take them back," He has to say, "and cleanse them again."

It would be a totally different matter if there were no Laver, no fountain, no provision for cleansing. This, indeed, would be a most serious matter. But, as the hymnwriter William Cowper (1731-1800) declared in 1772, "There is a fountain filled with blood." God has made every necessary provision so that we can come before Him cleansed, and we must not come before Him any other way. This is the message of the Bronze Laver, and it is the message of our Lord and Savior Jesus Christ. In His name and by His blood, we are washed, sanctified, and justified.

If you need to be cleansed today, if you need to be forgiven, look to Jesus. There are places that God wants to take you, but He can't take you there until you've gone by the Laver and been cleansed.

You need the new life of the born-again experience, and you need Jesus to take up residence within you. This is not just another philosophy or way of life. This is a relationship between you and God. And these are the things God wants to do in your life—if you will allow Him to do them.

Some would say, "Lord, I'm not worthy, for I have failed miserably," but you can walk in His worthiness. Because of Him, God will cleanse and forgive you. Begin your walk with God today. This is your day of cleansing. Take another giant step toward your divine encounter.

Chapter Five

THE TABLE OF SHOWBREAD

COMMUNION

You shall also make a table of acacia wood; two cubits shall be its length, a cubit its width, and a cubit and a half its height. And you shall overlay it with pure gold, and make a molding of gold all around. You shall make for it a frame of a handbreadth all around, and you shall make a gold molding for the frame all around. And you shall make for it four rings of gold, and put the rings on the four corners that are at its four legs. The rings shall be close to the frame, as holders for the poles to bear the table. And you shall make the poles of acacia wood, and overlay them with gold, that the table may be carried with them. You shall make its dishes, its pans, its pitchers, and its bowls for pouring. You shall make them of pure gold.

And you shall set the showbread on the table before Me always.
Exodus 25:23-30

And you shall take fine flour and bake twelve cakes with it, two-tenths of an ephah shall be in each cake. You shall set them in two rows, six in a row, on the pure gold table before the Lord. And you shall put pure frankincense on each row, that it may be on the bread for a memorial, an offering made by fire to the Lord. Every Sabbath he shall set it in order before the Lord continually, being taken from the children of Israel by an everlasting covenant. And it shall be for Aaron and his sons, and they shall eat it in a holy place; for it is most holy to him from the offerings of the Lord made by fire, by a perpetual statute. Leviticus 24:5-9

We have taken two very important steps toward your divine encounter, having been to both the Brazen Altar and the Bronze Laver, and having experienced both a substitutionary sacrifice and cleansing, and now we want to advance, going further into the divine, moving closer to God's presence.

In the Tabernacle, the next room was called the Holy Place, and there were located three more items of interest: the Table of Showbread, the Golden Candlestick, and the Altar of Incense. The first we come to is the Table of Showbread, or, as it was also called, the Table of Presence, or, simply, the Table of Bread.

Of all the furnishings in the Court, the Holy Place, and the Holy of Holies, this golden table, with its twelve loaves, or cakes, of bread, was the most difficult for me to understand. Since the bread on the table was provided for the priests and they ate it, a simple explanation could have been that it was merely there to nourish them while they went about their priestly duties. This was their lunch. But I was sure that there must have been more to it than that.

The Brazen Altar and the Laver had had significant and profound symbolic significance concerning our life today in God. Would the Lord take us so quickly from that level of spiritual insight to a mere lunch for the priests? Surely not!

If physical sustenance was all there was to the Table of Bread, why would God have made the priests wait seven days before they ate the bread? By that time, it was, no doubt, a little past its prime and quite possibly a little hard and crusty. If this bread was for nothing more than physical sustenance, it would seem that God had snatched the Table of Bread from among the profound and moved it into the mundane.

What did God really intend by the institution of the Table of Bread? What did it mean to Moses and the children of Israel? And what does it mean to us today? First, let us consider the construction of the table itself.

THE CONSTRUCTION OF THE TABLE

Three feet long, one and a half feet wide, and two and a quarter feet high, the table used for the Table of Showbread was, again, made from acacia wood. Then it was overlaid with pure gold, the most beautiful, durable, and valuable of all metals. As we have seen, the Brazen Altar and the Laver that were in the Court of the Tabernacle were made from brass. Now, God has called His people to move from brass to gold, from the Outer Court to the Holy Place, from the flesh into the Spirit, from the mundane into the supernatural.

There was a very good reason for the use of these particular metals. Brass was nice, but it was too common, for it was used for many common household utensils. It was fine for the furnishings in the area of the Tabernacle reserved for the common people, but now God was calling His people to move higher. The items located in the Holy Place must be covered by gold because this was a very restricted place, a place God had reserved for His presence. Everything there was either made from solid gold, or it was overlaid with gold.

When I think of metals and grades of metals, I immediately think of the bank cards being offered to consumers these days and also of some of the frequent-flyers' clubs and how they are ranked: silver, gold, and platinum. The purpose is clearly to cause the consumer to want to rise higher. It's always disappointing to be demoted from a higher category to a lower one, and most people try to either maintain their standing or to rise higher. And so it should be in our walk with the Lord. He wants us to be ever moving upward, ever closer to our miracle, ever closer to living in the realm of supernatural provision.

Higher! Closer! Deeper! This is our cry, and our constant goal...

Although we will never, in this life, cease to need forgiveness and cleansing, we should constantly seek to attain and then to maintain ever higher levels of spiritual and moral excellence in our walk with the Lord. Every believer should strive to go from one level of grace to another. This was clearly the goal of the apostle Paul, who wrote:

Not that I have already attained, or am already perfected; but I press on, that I may lay hold of that for which Christ Jesus has also laid hold of me. Brethren, I do not count myself to have apprehended; but one thing I do, forgetting those things which are behind and reaching forward to those things which are ahead, I press toward the goal for the prize of the upward call of God in Christ Jesus. Philippians 3:12-14

It is one thing to need periodic visits to the Brass Laver, but it would not be good for any one of us to live there permanently or to be sent back from the Holy Place because we had done something that required more cleansing. Let us climb ever higher and not be slipping back.

Sadly, many of those who accept the Lord Jesus as their Savior are no more mature spiritually years later than they were the day they got saved. This ought not to be! With all of the resources available to us, we should never be today where we were years ago. Let us climb higher. Let us get closer to God. Let us move on into His presence.

Higher! Closer! Deeper! This is our cry, and our constant goal—to know the Lord better with every day that passes. It's time to move on up.

The fact that the Table of Showbread was made both of wood and of gold is significant. The wood in it symbolized the human dimension, and the gold in it symbolized the divine. The table thus symbolized the coming together of, or the interaction of, the human and the divine: man and God together in communion.

The table also symbolized Jesus, the Son of God, because He took on humanity that He might present us before our holy Father God. He was, at the very same time, both human and divine.

It should also be noted that there was (according to Exodus 25:25) a frame, a band, an elevated edge around the top of the table. This band was designed to keep the special bread that was placed on the table from falling off of it. In that day, the people of Israel were the bread, and now, we, as believers in Christ, are the bread. And God has put some mechanisms and some provisions in place to keep us from falling from the Lord's table.

Jude wrote:

Now unto him that is able to keep you from falling, and to present you faultless before the presence of his glory with exceeding joy... Jude 24

Paul wrote to Timothy:

For the which cause I also suffer these things: nevertheless I am not ashamed: for I know whom I have believed, and am persuaded that he is able to keep that which I have committed unto him against that day. 2 Timothy 1:12

Jesus Himself said:

My sheep hear my voice, and I know them, and they follow me: and I give unto them eternal life; and they shall never perish, neither shall any man pluck them out of my hand. My Father, which gave them me, is greater than all; and no man is able to pluck them out of my Father's hand. I and my Father are one. John 10:27-30

This special band around the Table of Showbread was described as *"of a handbreadth,"* or about the width of a man's hand. This shows us that God has His hands around us protecting us at every moment and in every situation.

Many Christians are worried about their spiritual survival, about the possibility of slipping over the edge. But God does not want us to be worried and anxious about anything:

For God has not given us a spirit of fear, but of power and of love and of a sound mind. 2 Timothy 1:7

God has given us an assurance of salvation, an assurance of eternal life, and we need not be afraid of losing it. If you do slip over the edge and fall, it will be because you wanted to. In order to fall, you will have to literally climb over all of the things God has designed to keep and sustain you and to prevent this very thing from happening. In that case, you will have no one but yourself to blame.

Some believers love to live on the edge, but that's always a dangerous and foolish game to play. How far can you get from God and still be *in* God? The fact that you are even asking the question shows that your soul is in danger. One of these times, you'll slip off the edge.

How close can I get to God? How much can I do for Him? How much can I praise Him? This is the attitude to have, and when you have it, you are protected and sustained.

WHAT WAS THE SHOWBREAD
AND WHAT DID IT MEAN?

God called the bread that was offered on the table *"showbread,"* which meant "bread of the faces" or "bread of the presence." He specifically stated that He wanted this bread to be in its place on this table in the Holy Place *"continually,"* or *"always"* (*"set it in order before the LORD continually,"* Leviticus 24:8, *"And you shall set the showbread on the table before Me always,"* Exodus 25:30). Because of this, the priests developed an elaborate system for removing and replacing the bread on the table so that the space occupied by each loaf of bread would be empty for absolutely the least amount of time possible. A priest standing on one side of the table would begin to lift a loaf of bread to remove it, and another priest standing on the other side of the table would put a new loaf in its place immediately.

Most Bible commentators have felt that the twelve loaves of bread on the Table of Showbread represented the twelve tribes of Israel, and that they thus communicated God's desire to dwell with His people constantly and His desire that His people should dwell with Him, both collectively and individually. The implication of this is that God is present with His people, and that they are constantly before His face. This is a privilege that is even more available to believers today. At the same time, it is an obligation. God said in His Word:

> *And let us consider one another in order to stir up love and good works, not forsaking the assembling of ourselves together, as is the manner of some, but exhorting one another, and so much the more as you see the Day approaching.* Hebrews 10:24-25

Going to church and gathering with the people of the Lord is not an option that we can take or leave as we see fit. It is compulsory. This is not something we do when we feel like it or when we want to, and therefore it is not something that we can avoid if we don't feel like doing it. Regular church attendance is something that we should and must do.

It's interesting: some people can do things for anyone and everyone else but God. For example, we go to work when we are sick and when we are tired because we don't want to lose the pay. It doesn't matter how upset or depressed we are, we go to work anyway. Yet we count any and all of these conditions as legitimate excuses for not going to church.

David said:

> *I was glad when they said to me, "Let us go into the house of the Lord."* Psalm 122:1

Even after ten of the twelve tribes of Israel had split off from the rest, forming the northern kingdom (Israel), and only two tribes remained in the southern kingdom (Judah), the priests continued to place twelve loaves of bread on the Table, as if these loaves represented a prayer for unity. If there is one thing we desperately need in the Church today it is unity among brothers.

There is a sense in which we should go before the Lord not just individually, but as a part of the church collectively, not just thinking of "me" and of "I," but of "we" and of "us." Sadly, few Christians are thinking "we" and "us," and most are thinking "me," "I," and "my."

God has placed us in this thing together, and unless and until we can begin to think collectively, we will not be where He wants us to be. We should seek to come together before God, not just in terms of our physical presence, but also with a togetherness of heart.

The Tabernacle was, at times, referred to as *"the tabernacle of meeting."* What was done there was for all of us collectively and for each of us individually. It was not just about the place; it was about each of us entering into a personal relationship with the Spirit of God and into a relationship with one another.

But communion with one another begins with a proper communion with God. The psalmist declared:

As the deer pants for the water brooks, so pants my soul for You, O God. My soul thirsts for God, for the living God. When shall I come and appear before God? Psalm 42:1-2

Without a genuine thirst for God, we are nothing. Being in one building together, sometimes thousands of us focused on the same thing, is a wonderful experience. Enjoying the good music together is wonderful, and sharing together in many other ways is also wonderful. But the basis of our coming together must always be our hunger for God. Entering into His presence and being ministered to by His Spirit must be at the very top of our agenda.

THE ORDER OF THE BREAD

This bread was not just thrown onto the table or even placed there haphazardly. It was to be *"set in order ... before the Lord."* This shows us the importance of order in our own personal lives and of order in the Body of Christ as a whole. Each of us should be set in his or her place and functioning where we are placed:

> *For by one Spirit we were all baptized into one body—whether Jews or Greeks, whether slaves or free—and have all been made to drink into one Spirit. For in fact the body is not one member but many.* 1 Corinthians 12:13-14

When you make a commitment in the local church, please keep your commitment. You have made it not only to man, but also to God. After all, it's His Church. If you make a promise, then keep your promise. You haven't made it only to man, but also to God. If you say you will be somewhere, then be there.

Other people order their lives around what you say, and if you don't follow through, you become a hindrance to many others. Others order their lives around your designated function, and if you fail to carry out that function, these other people are also negatively affected. If God has placed you in a certain role, others assume that you will be faithful in that role. They depend on that fact, and when you fail, you cause heartache in the lives of many others.

The Lord has a place for every single one of us in His work. Find your place, and be faithful in it. Begin to recognize that you are part of a whole, and if you are not functioning properly, the whole is adversely affected. No man is an island, and no man walks alone.

> *Each man's joy is joy to me.*
> *Each man's grief is my own.*
> *We need one another,*
> *So I will defend each man as my brother*
> *And each man as my friend.*

Paul wrote:

Now you are the body of Christ, and members individually. 1
Corinthians 12:27

Each member of the Body, just as each loaf of bread, has its place
and its role. Why is it that so many refuse to take their rightful place or
to play their designated role?

WAS THE SHOWBREAD LEAVENED OR UNLEAVENED?

Was the Showbread leavened or unleavened? Not all historians agree
on this point. Josephus, the famous Jewish historian, stated that the
loaves for the table were made *without* leaven. This would seem consis-
tent with the teachings of the apostle Paul, who, in the New Testament,
compared believers with bread and strongly stated that we must be
without leaven, leaven being a symbol of corruption:

> *Your glorying is not good. Do you not know that a little leaven leav-
> ens the whole lump? Therefore purge out the old leaven, that you
> may be a new lump, since you truly are unleavened. For indeed
> Christ, our Passover, was sacrificed for us. Therefore let us keep the
> feast, not with old leaven, nor with the leaven of malice and
> wickedness, but with the unleavened bread of sincerity and truth.* 1
> Corinthians 5:6-8

> *A little leaven leavens the whole lump.* Galatians 5:9

Everything in the Tabernacle was made according to a heavenly pattern, and there is no sin in heaven. This, again, leads us to conclude that
the bread of the Tabernacle would certainly have been made *without*
leaven.

For the few who might not understand the term "leaven," it is a substance that causes fermentation, and therefore expansion, in bread

dough or batter. For bread-making purposes, leaven was actually little more than fermented dough. Some of it was held over, and when it was mixed with a new batch of dough, it produced fermentation in it as well.

The fermentation process is caused by any one of a group of yeasts, molds, and bacteria (yeast actually being a fungus). The term *fermentation* has also come to have other unrelated meanings: "agitation, unrest, or excitement."

Physical fermentation has several levels. The first is a simple expansion, the puffing up, or rising of the dough. Some of this is desirable, but be careful. Too much fermentation has an ugly consequence. The last phase of fermentation is actual decay. Watch out when people start puffing up; they may be headed for decay and disintegration.

Pull your nose down out of the air and walk in humility because God has promised to exalt the humble, but He will bring down those who exalt themselves:

For whoever exalts himself will be humbled, and he who humbles himself will be exalted. Luke 14:11

As we have seen in a previous chapter, Paul wrote to the Corinthian believers urging them not to corrupted by their surroundings:

Therefore, having these promises, beloved, let us cleanse ourselves from all filthiness of the flesh and spirit, perfecting holiness in the fear of God. 2 Corinthians 7:1

A similar plea was sent to the believers in Rome:

I beseech you therefore, brethren, by the mercies of God, that you present your bodies a living sacrifice, holy, acceptable to God, which is your reasonable service. And do not be conformed to this world, but be transformed by the renewing of your mind, that you may prove what is that good and acceptable and perfect will of God. Romans 12:1-2

The Showbread represented the very best the people could offer to God.

༄༅

The bread on the Table of Bread was surely unleavened, and this speaks to us that we should come clean and righteous before the Lord. Far too many come any old way, and this is not pleasing to God. Paul wrote to the Romans:

Shall we continue in sin that grace may abound? Certainly not! How shall we who died to sin live any longer in it? Romans 6:1-2

The King James Version says it a little stronger:

God forbid.

Paul went on:

Reckon yourselves to be dead indeed to sin, but alive to God in Christ Jesus our Lord. Romans 6:11

God wants us to come before Him, but we must come before Him clean and righteous. We have been by the Altar, and an atonement has been made. We have been by the Laver, and our sins have been washed away. We have been allowed into the Holy Place, and we must stand as the bread on the Golden Table clean before the Lord our God.

OFFERING GOD THE VERY BEST

The Showbread represented the very best the people could offer to God. Their supply of wheat, and thus of bread made from wheat, was very limited during their years of wandering in the wilderness (which was also the earliest time of the Tabernacle). The people themselves ate manna, heavenly bread, for sustenance, but they offered their available earthly bread to the Lord. They could have said, "Let us offer to the Lord that which is plentiful, not that which is scarce." But although bread was so scarce, they gave it to the Lord. Or, better said, *because* bread was so scarce, they gave it to the Lord.

The very presence of the children of Israel in Egypt in the first place had been caused by a scarcity of bread. Because of an impending famine all over the then-known world, God had miraculously positioned Joseph in Egypt to save the people. It was in this way that the children of Israel (literally the children and grandchildren of Israel, who was formerly known as Jacob) were brought into Egypt, and it was in this way that bread was provided for them during the time of famine.

After the death of Joseph, a pharaoh who had not known him enslaved the children of Israel, and many centuries later they had to be delivered from Egypt. Now, on their way back to their own land, they again faced a shortage of wheat, and, consequently, of bread. God provided food for them by sending manna down from heaven each morning, but it was under these dire circumstances, there in a barren wilderness, that God required them to provide the Showbread for the Tabernacle.

In order to provide the required Showbread, they would have to find enough wheat, thresh it and preserve it, so that every week there would be enough loaves for the Table of Bread. God knew that there was a shortage of wheat, but He asked the people to do this for Him, and He promised that if they would do it, He would take care of them. That's His promise to you too.

The Showbread could not be made with just any flour; it had to be made from *"fine flour."* This implies the use of only the best grains available, ground to a fine point and baked in such a way that it would make the best possible bread. In return, God gave His people His very best— manna from heaven.

What was this *"manna"*?

Now the manna was like coriander seed, and its color like the color of bdellium. The people went about and gathered it, ground it on millstones or beat it in the mortar, cooked it in pans, and made cakes of it; and its taste was like the taste of pastry prepared with oil. And when the dew fell on the camp in the night, the manna fell on it. Numbers 11:7-9

The manna God sent sounds almost like cake to me. It was not only nutritionally sound and balanced, but it was also pleasing to the taste.

The people were to gather an omer (about two quarts) of it each day per person, and on the sixth day they gathered two omers (about a gallon), one extra omer for the Sabbath-day portion. In the same way, each loaf of bread for the Table of Showbread had two omers of flour in it. Those loaves, then, represented a Sabbath-day portion.

As the people offered God flour from which their coveted cakes were made, this was an expression of their faith that He would continue to provide for them. In the same way, when we give to the Lord and His work today in generosity, we do so because He has provided for us, but also because we know that He *will* provide for us in the future.

To some, I rather imagine, this custom of placing a fine quality bread in the Tabernacle might have seemed like a trick by the priests to have the best for themselves while everybody else was eating manna. But the description of the manna makes me know that God's least is always better than our best. The manna was better than any bread man could prepare. And, since each of us is a priest in these New Testament times, we cannot complain about the privilege of the priests.

It was only right for the priests to consume the bread after it had been before the Lord for seven days, because when you consume a substance, you become that substance, and that substance becomes you. You are what you eat, for you become identified with it, and it becomes identified with you. As each priest went to the Golden Altar, and as the High Priest went through the Veil and before the Mercy Seat, he carried with him the children of Israel because he had eaten the bread that represented them. The priests' eating of the loaves, therefore, was a sign of God's acceptance of His people.

We should also remember an incident in the life of Elijah:

And it came to pass after a while, that the brook dried up, because there had been no rain in the land. And the word of the Lord came unto him, saying, Arise, get thee to Zarephath, which belongeth to Zidon, and dwell there: behold, I have commanded a widow woman there to sustain thee. So he arose and went to Zarephath. And when he came to the gate of the city, behold, the widow woman was there gathering of sticks: and he called to her, and said, Fetch me, I pray thee, a little water in a vessel, that I may drink. And as she was going to fetch it, he called to her, and said, Bring me, I pray thee, a morsel of bread in thine hand. And she said, As the Lord thy God liveth, I have not a cake, but an handful of meal in a barrel, and a little oil in a cruse: and, behold, I am gathering two sticks, that I may go in and dress it for me and my son, that we may eat it, and die.

And Elijah said unto her, Fear not; go and do as thou hast said: but make me thereof a little cake first, and bring it unto me, and after make for thee and for thy son. For thus saith the Lord God of Israel, The barrel of meal shall not waste, neither shall the cruse of oil fail, until the day that the Lord sendeth rain upon the earth. And she went and did according to the saying of Elijah: and she, and he, and her house, did eat many days. And the barrel of meal wasted not, neither did the cruse of oil fail, according to the word of the Lord, which he spake by Elijah. 1 Kings 17:7-16, KJV

If I had been there that day, I might not have treated Elijah well. Imagine taking the last meal from a poor widow! But this was God's way of providing for the woman and her son.

When Elijah spoke those words, *"The barrel of meal shall not waste, neither shall the cruise of oil fail,"* faith began to rise in the woman's heart, and she went to prepare Elijah a meal. As she was preparing the meal for the prophet, she wasn't doing it for the man of God; she was doing it for the God of the man. And, after she had done it and looked again into the barrel, there was more meal in it than there had been before she started. There was also more oil in the cruise than there had been before. This miracle continued to happen for her every single day until the famine had ended. Child of God, when you take care of God's business, He *will* take care of yours—always.

When you say no to God and give in to your own fleshly desires, you are shortchanging yourself. If you put yourself ahead of God, you can expect shortage in your life. But when you put God first, you can expect His miraculous supply to come to you. Jesus promised:

When you say no to God and give in to your own fleshly desires, you are shortchanging yourself.

But seek first the kingdom of God and His righteousness, and all these things shall be added to you. Matthew 6:33

When you seek Him *first*, He gets busy on your behalf and starts adding *"things"* to your life. He refuses to allow you to make a sacrifice without receiving His blessing in return for it.

All God asked the people for was twelve loaves of bread per week on the Table, and if they would be faithful in providing those loaves, He would send them enough manna to feed them and their families every single day of their lives. That was a pretty good trade off. A little sacrifice resulted in a whole lot of blessing. They gave the Lord bread from the earth, and He gave them bread from heaven.

Bread represents the harvest of seeds that have been sown, the fruit of man's labor (always remember that it is God who gives the increase). When we give that which is the fruit of our labors and our time, it is as if we are giving ourselves, our very life. When we give that which we could have consumed or enjoyed, we are investing in our covenant with God, because covenants are sealed by an exchange of tokens.

THE MANNA AND THE SHOWBREAD AS SHADOWS OF CHRIST

The manna was, in many ways, symbolic of Jesus Christ, the Son of God:

They said to Him, "... Our fathers ate the manna in the desert; as it is written, 'He gave them bread from heaven to eat.'"

Then Jesus said to them, "Most assuredly, I say to you, Moses did not give you the bread from heaven, but My Father gives you the true bread from heaven. For the bread of God is He who comes down from heaven and gives life to the world.

Then they said to Him, "Lord, give us this bread always."

And Jesus said to them, "I am the bread of life. He who comes to Me shall never hunger, and he who believes in Me shall never thirst. John 6:31-35

When they rejected Him, Jesus later said to them:

"For My flesh is food indeed, and My blood is drink indeed. He who eats My flesh and drinks My blood abides in Me, and I in him." John 6:55-56

This does not refer to cannibalism. To eat Christ's flesh is to come to him, and to drink of His blood is to believe on Him. If you can come to Jesus and believe on Him, you are guaranteed everlasting life.

Although it is the manna which is more clearly the symbol of Jesus, He shares much in common with the bread on the table—because Jesus suffered, and everything about bread denotes suffering.

A grain of wheat is cast into the cold ground, and there it has to die so that it can give birth to a small shoot. That tender shoot has to break through the crust of the ground to face the cold of winter or the heat of summer. It is subsequently assailed by wind and rain. This denotes suffering.

Then, when the plant has grown and matured, the stalks of wheat will have to be cut with a sharp sickle and then threshed to separate husk from kernel. This denotes suffering.

The gleaned kernels are then ground into flour, which is then kneaded into dough and then cast into a hot oven until it is golden brown. This denotes suffering.

Finally, the bread is broken and consumed to satiate the hunger of men. This denotes suffering.

Our Lord left the comforts of heaven for the challenges of earth. He was born in relative poverty and lived His early life in obscurity. He tried to help the world, but it rejected Him and ultimately hung Him on a rugged cross. Nails were driven into His hands and feet. He hung there until He was dead. This denotes suffering.

He was cast into a cruel grave, but thank God, three days later, He arose:

God has highly exalted Him and given Him the name which is above every name, that at the name of Jesus, every knee should bow ... and that every tongue should confess that Jesus Christ is Lord.
Philippians 2:9

Jesus took the bread of communion in His hand and said, *"This is My body"* (Matthew 26:26), and again Paul tells us that we are *"the body of Christ, and members in particular"* (1 Corinthians 12:27, KJV). So in a sense Jesus is bread to us, and we are bread to Him. Maybe this is why He said, *"If you abide in Me, and My words abide in you, you will ask what you desire, and it will be done for you"* (John 15:7).

THE FRANKINCENSE ON THE TABLE

Each time the Showbread was put in place frankincense was placed in small golden bowls on top of each stack or line of six loaves. The frankincense thus came into association with the bread, and association with a thing implies taking on its nature. The incense, having been placed on the bread, took on the nature of the bread, so that it could be offered up in place of the bread.

At the end of the seven days, just before the bread was replaced (or just as it was being replaced), the bowl of frankincense was lifted from the Table of Bread and carried to the Golden Altar, or Altar of Incense. Sprinkled over the fire of the Altar, it was soon consumed, and the aroma of it rose up to fill the Holy Place.

The Frankincense, first of all, symbolizes Jesus. He associated Himself with us, being born as a man, and then He took upon Himself our transgressions and the punishment for our sins. Having associated Himself with us and taken our suffering upon Himself, Jesus ascended back unto the Father on high. Even now, He is there making intercession for us. The Frankincense also symbolizes prayer offered up before God, and it symbolizes worship and praise.

Frankincense is a very distasteful substance, often described as nauseating, but when it is placed in the fire it produces a very fragrant aroma. It is only when we have gone through the fire that the best comes out of us. Our sometimes bitter experiences can bring forth something very pleasant—when they have been subjected to God's fire.

The people of Moses' day went to the Brazen Altar, where sacrifices were offered for their sins. They went to the Laver and were cleansed. Then, as bread, they went inside the Holy Place and presented themselves continually before the face of the Lord. After that, the incense of their praise offered up a sweet fragrance unto Him.

In the same sense, we go to the cross of Jesus Christ with our sins where His blood purchases our forgiveness, and the water our cleansing. Then we go to the Laver where we cleanse ourselves of all filthiness of the flesh and spirit. We then go into the Holy Place where we abide on the Table of God's Presence. Then we offer up the incense of our praise to Him who is worthy of all praise.

So the burning of the incense was a symbol of praise and worship, and praise and worship (as we will see in Chapters 7 and 8) is what we were born to do. Worship is not just for the church choir or for those we have designated as "the praise team." It's for every child of God. Every single one of us should be offering up praise unto the Lord.

We praise God for what He has done. He has done great things for us, and we're glad about it. So, we need to give Him the glory due unto

His name. If He never again does another thing for us, He has already done so much that we cannot help but praise Him for the rest of our lives.

We also praise God for who He is. He is the mighty God. He is the holy God. He is the omnipresent, omnipotent God. He's a God of love and a God of mercy.

We praise God because praise lifts our spirits. If you are discouraged or depressed, don't just sit there in that condition. Begin to praise God, and the more you praise Him, the better you'll feel. The more you praise Him the higher He'll lift you.

We praise God because praise is the expression of our faith. When you have faith, you don't look at things as they now are, but as they will soon be. If you have faith, you don't look at your predicament, but you praise God because He will bring you out of your predicament. And the more you praise Him, the stronger your faith will become. God will work it out, and He will bring you out.

We praise God because praise defeats the enemy:

Now when they [Jehoshaphat and the people] *began to sing and to praise, the Lord set ambushes against the people of Ammon, Moab, and Mount Seir, who had come against Judah; and they were defeated.* 2 Chronicles 20:22

The more you praise God, the more He will work for you.

We praise God because He inhabits the praises of His people. When you praise Him, you fashion a throne He can sit on, and He never fails to occupy such a throne. From there, He dispenses blessings, sending forth miracles and healings for His people. The more you praise Him, the more elaborate the throne becomes that you provide for Him. And, as you praise Him, He has promised to bring you up and bring you out.

We praise God because He is worthy of our praise. He is worthy of honor, worthy of glory. So throw back your head, open your mouth, and praise Him today. More will be said on this all-important subject when we get to Chapters 7 and 8.

You have taken several very important steps toward your divine encounter, but several more remain. Don't stop now. Press forward.

Chapter Six

THE LAMPSTAND
ENLIGHTENMENT

You shall also make a lampstand of pure gold; the lampstand shall be of hammered work. Its shaft, its branches, its bowls, its ornamental knobs, and flowers shall be of one piece. And six branches shall come out of its sides: three branches of the lampstand out of one side, and three branches of the lampstand out of the other side.

You shall make seven lamps for it, and they shall arrange its lamps so that they give light in front of it. And its wick-trimmers and their trays shall be of pure gold. It shall be made of a talent of pure gold, with all these utensils. And see to it that you make them according to the pattern which was shown you on the mountain. Exodus 25:31-32 and 37-40

We're ready for the next step into divine encounter, and it is accomplished at the Lampstand. This beautiful and yet practical creation, known to the Israelis as the Menora, holds a wealth of blessing for us. Nothing could be more important to us than light. We want to be fully enlightened.

Some translations of the Bible, including the King James Version, call this object found in the Holy Place *"the Candlestick,"* but it could not have been a candlestick because it had no candles. The Lampstand actually consisted of seven oil-fueled lamps. One flame burned in the middle branch, and separate flames burned on each of three branches on either side of it. There were, then, seven flames, producing seven lights. That represents perfect, or full, enlightenment. I like that, for we need all the light we can get in this Christian life!

An experience I had in Nigeria serves to illustrate this fact. A large group of our people accompanied me on a two-week ministry trip to Ghana and Nigeria. Things went extremely well for us, and we were able to accomplish several important objectives and to meet some very special and precious people. The last leg of the trip was spent in Abuja, Nigeria. There, the president of Nigeria, His Excellency President Obasanjo, was kind enough to invite us to one of his daily seven a.m. prayer sessions.

I was determined not to be late for that meeting, so I got up before five o'clock. It was still dark outside, and even darker in my hotel room, and just as I started to get ready, the lights went out. It was a beautiful hotel, belonging to a well known chain, but the lights had failed in the entire area, so there was nothing the hotel could do.

I had not yet showered or shaved, or even selected a suit and tie (or any other item of clothing) to wear that day, and now there I was in total darkness. I had no flashlight, no matches, and no candle, but I decided to try to do it all in the dark—even though I could barely find my way around the room.

How could I find my razor and the other items I needed? I wondered. I groped and stumbled around until I found my shaving kit, and was amazed when I was able to shave under those difficult conditions. But it had taken much too long, and I was sure I would not be ready on time without some light. "Please, Lord, let the lights come on," I prayed, and a moment later they came back on.

Some will say that the lights were going to come on anyway. Well, maybe so. And, then, maybe not. Maybe they came on because I prayed. Regardless of the reason they came on, I had to give the Lord the praise. It was so much easier for me to wash and dress in the light than it would have been in the dark.

In our lighted modern world, it is difficult for us to imagine how significant light was to ancient men. We have gained such scientific mastery over our environment that the wheels of commerce and industry can now continue to turn at night just as they do in the daytime. This, however, is a purely modern phenomenon.

WHAT LIGHT MEANT TO ANCIENT MAN

With the marvels of modern science, we can now change the blackness of the midnight into the brightness of noonday with a flick of the switch. We can pierce the curtain of darkness with our high powered auto headlights and prepare a path of light along which we can drive at high speeds at night. We can penetrate the murkiness and illuminate faraway objects, which have been otherwise hidden by the night.

For ancient men, the situation was very different. He did not have the ability to modify the darkness and to light up the night as we do. Night and darkness, therefore, were a terror for him. There was the always-present danger of being attacked by wild beasts, and many other unseen hazards of the night—robbers being one of the greatest of them. There was also the possibility of losing one's way. Beyond those very real dangers were the superstitious fears ancient men had about countless spirits and demons that did their devilment under the cloak of darkness.

Unless it was absolutely impossible to do so, ancient men ceased all activity at or shortly before nightfall and then retreated to the relative safety of their dwellings. There they tended to their fires or trimmed their oil lamps to make sure they would burn throughout the night.

Although the ancients did have different words for light and fire, for them light *was* fire. Therefore, the control of fire was one of the most, if not *the* most, significant achievements of ancient times. And it did not come easily. They had to use crude flint rocks, rub dry sticks together, or start a fire from an already existing fire. The latter method was always easiest and best—when it was possible.

Fire not only represented light; it also represented warmth and protection. It was used for cooking food, and it served a variety of other purposes. In certain organized ancient societies, one of the most important individuals, therefore, was the keeper of the flame. When all fires had gone out, a family could often go to him and get fire to restart their own flames.

For those who lived during biblical times, a lamp of some type was a great necessity in the home. Not having matches to strike (and often not having a keeper of the flame to go to), families had to keep a fire burning which could be used to light any other fires they would need in and around the home. Only the poorest of people, therefore, slept without a lamp burning, and the absence of a lamp burning at night in any dwelling meant either extreme poverty or the absence of life.

One of the most terrible curses of the ancient world was to predict that a person's light would be put out. Thus, Job's accuser, Bildad, could say:

The light of the wicked indeed goes out, and the flame of his fire does not shine. The light is dark in his tent, and his lamp beside him is put out. Job 18:5-6

If a lamp was put out, all sorts of evil could befall the family. At the very least, if all of a family's lamps were allowed to go out, a great effort would have to be expended to restart a fire, or someone would have to be sent many miles to obtain fire from someone else. It was so much easier to keep a fire burning than to start one from scratch.

Although light is much more easily accessible to us in this day, it is just as important as ever. We simply cannot do without it. Given these conditions, it is easy to understand why, over the centuries, darkness and night came to be associated with certain unpleasant and sorrowful aspects of life. Darkness indicated trouble, just as brightness represented good fortune and happiness.

When the Bible speaks of darkness, it is not always referring to nighttime, but rather to those situations in which man finds that he cannot see his way, is without guidance, or is lost. Darkness refers to those times when invisible monsters and enemies terrorize man, when his existence seems to be filled with danger, when he is blinded to right and wrong and has no moral light to guide him.

> *Fire, and thus, light, came to represent God, and He often manifested Himself to man through fire.*

All of us have known a darkness that had nothing to do with the position of the sun, and our darkest nights sometimes come at the brightest moments of the noonday. Conversely, all of us have walked in the sunlight while our hearts and minds were in the shadows. We know what it is to wonder if the future will be bright. "The outlook is dark," many would say, but from the beginning of time, our God has been a God of light:

> *In the beginning God created the heavens and the earth. The earth was without form, and void; and darkness was on the face of the deep. And the Spirit of God was hovering over the face of the waters. Then God said, "Let there be light"; and there was light. And God saw the light, that it was good; and God divided the light from the darkness. God called the light Day, and the darkness He called Night. So the evening and the morning were the first day. Genesis 1:1-5*

Fire, and thus, light, came to represent God, and He often manifested Himself to man through fire. It was fire that God attracted Moses' attention at Mt. Horeb, where he saw a bush that burned all day and yet was not consumed:

ENCOUNTERING GOD

And the Angel of the Lord appeared to him in a flame of fire from the midst of a bush. Exodus 3:2

After God had delivered His children from bondage in Egypt, He again manifested His presence by fire:

And the Lord went before them by day in a pillar of cloud to lead the way, and by night in a pillar of fire to give them light, so as to go by day and night. He did not take away the pillar of cloud by day or the pillar of fire by night from before the people. Exodus 13:21-22

Thus the children of Israel did not have to worry about light to lighten their way at night, about coats to warm them from the cold, or about being protected from their enemies. God's fire provided them light to lighten the way, fire to warm them, and it served as a wall of separation between them and their enemies, protecting them.

Later, after the Tabernacle was constructed, Moses anointed five priests to the ministry, Aaron and his four sons. These priests were consecrated and anointed, and Moses sent them into the Tabernacle for seven days of separation and consecration to God. On the ninth day following their consecration, the priests came forth to offer sacrifices for themselves and for the people. While these sacrifices were burning upon the altar, Moses and Aaron came forth to bless the people. At that time, the glory of the Lord appeared, and His presence was again manifested by fire:

And fire came out from before the Lord and consumed the burnt offering and the fat on the altar. When all the people saw it, they shouted and fell on their faces. Leviticus 9:24

Fire had been kindled upon the altar prior to this time, but this fire was different; it came down out of heaven. It was the fire of God's presence, and it sanctified, consecrated, and imparted its nature to the fire that was already burning on the altar. The fire from heaven merged and mixed itself with the fire on the altar and gave it a new nature. This is why God commanded His people, *"The fire shall ever be burning upon the altar; it shall never go out"* (Leviticus 6:13, KJV). This fire was unlike any other fire known to man, so it must always be kept properly fueled.

The ever-burning fire on the altar symbolized God's acceptance of the sacrifices of the people, His favor, His forgiveness, His presence, His power, His purity, and His holiness. It symbolized the continual worship of the people of God and their never-dying zeal to do His will.

God sent the fire, but He commanded the people to keep it burning upon the altar. The fire was His, but it was to be fueled by the common olive oil of the people.

God's fire alone was to be used in His service and His worship, and any other ceremonial fire was to be started from the fire that He had sent. His fire alone was to be used to light the seven flames of the Lampstand, as well as the fire on the Altar of Incense. In a very real sense, God again provided light for His children—this time in the Tabernacle.

The Menora speaks to us of the Holy Spirit, who was sent into the world to enlighten believers:

> *However, when He, the Spirit of truth, has come, He will guide you into all truth; for He will not speak on His own authority, but whatever He hears He will speak; and He will tell you things to come.* John 16:13

It is at the Candlestick that we receive revelation and where we enter into the prophetic realm.

The Lampstand speaks to us of the Word of God, which is given to us for our enlightenment. David recognized this when he said:

> *Your word is a lamp to my feet and a light to my path.* Psalm 119:105

In this one psalm, David spoke of the power of the Word of God over and over again. For instance:

> *So shall I have an answer for him who reproaches me, for I trust in Your word.* Psalm 119:42

Direct my steps by Your word, and let no iniquity have dominion over me. Psalm 119:133

This truth, that God's Word enlightens our lives, is repeated over and over again throughout the Scriptures.

There are other truths spoken to us by the Lampstand, but first, let us look briefly at its construction.

THE CONSTRUCTION OF THE LAMPSTAND

The Lampstand, with its branches, was made from pure gold. It was not poured into a mold, but rather it was hammered into the desired shape. The stand weighed about a hundred pounds or more, and its makeup presents many metaphors and symbols to us, speaking to us of many things.

On each branch of the Lampstand were golden images of buds, flowers, and fruit from the almond tree. Thus, the Lampstand was an expression of God's grace and mercy extended to the High Priest, Aaron, and to his sons who were the priests of God. Here's why that is true:

As we have seen, at one point, there was a series of rebellions against the leadership of Moses and Aaron. When the first of these occurred, the ground opened up and swallowed the tents of three of the leaders of the rebellion. Then two hundred and fifty of those who had participated in the rebellion were destroyed by fire from heaven. Still, some had not yet learned their lesson. They began to murmur and complain, and the result was that a plague came upon them, and fourteen thousand seven hundred people died.

Eventually, in order to end all further insurrection, the Lord instructed Moses to take the twelve rods and place the name of one of the twelve tribes of Israel on each of them. On the twelfth rod, he placed the name Aaron, as representative of the tribe of Levi. Then the rods were placed in the Tabernacle and left overnight. Then, as we saw in Chapter 1, something wonderful happened:

Now it came to pass on the next day that Moses went into the tabernacle of witness, and behold, the rod of Aaron, of the house of Levi, had sprouted and put forth buds, had produced blossoms and yielded ripe almonds. Then Moses brought out all the rods from before the Lord to all the children of Israel; and they looked, and each man took his rod. And the Lord said to Moses, "Bring Aaron's rod back before the Testimony, to be kept as a sign against the rebels, that you may put their complaints away from Me, lest they die."
Numbers 17:8-10

Of the twelve, Aaron's rod was the only one that sprouted and put forth buds, flowers, and ripe almonds, and the amazing thing was that it all happened in one night. This was God's way of saying, "Aaron is My chosen and anointed High Priest, and I will stand behind him and support him against any rebellion."

Therefore, the Lampstand, with its buds, flowers, and fruit from the almond tree on each branch, was a reminder to the Israelites to respect their leaders in the role assigned to them. It was a reminder to Aaron and the other priests that they were what they were only because God had chosen them.

This was nothing but the grace of God because Aaron had, at times, proven to be a weak-willed and impulsive person. While Moses was on the mountain receiving the Law, Aaron allowed the people to talk him into fashioning an idol for them to worship (see Exodus 32). On another occasion, he and his sister Miriam criticized Moses for marrying a black woman (see Numbers 12). Miriam was stricken with leprosy because of it. Still, despite Aaron's poor record, God chose him, and then He worked wonderful miracles for and through him.

None of us deserves the blessings of God, and He would have every justification for passing us over. Thank God that in His great love, He has chosen us anyway.

When God does choose you for a position of leadership among His people, you won't have to argue, fuss, and fight to fulfill your role. If

God has chosen you, He will make your rod to bud, blossom, and bear fruit for all to see. So, every time Aaron and the priests went into the Holy Place and looked at the candlestick, they were reminded of the amazing grace of God.

...the Lampstand is a symbol of hope to us and also a symbol of the resurrection of our Lord Jesus Christ.

The almond was the first of all the trees in Palestine to bud and to blossom each season. It showed forth new life when all other trees were still standing dormant. Therefore, this tree became a symbol of resurrection and hope. Because of this, the Lampstand is a symbol of hope to us and also a symbol of the resurrection of our Lord Jesus Christ.

THE LAMPSTAND SPEAKS OF JESUS

The Lampstand speaks of Jesus in other ways as well. It was made from hammered gold, and Jesus had nails hammered through His hands and feet:

Surely He has borne our griefs and carried our sorrows; yet we esteemed Him stricken, smitten by God, and afflicted. But He was wounded for our transgressions, He was bruised for our iniquities; the chastisement for our peace was upon Him, and by His stripes we are healed. Isaiah 53:4-5

The Lampstand was not just hammered; it was hammered gold. Again, that speaks to us of Jesus. John said of Him:

And the Word became flesh and dwelt among us, and we beheld His glory, the glory as of the only begotten of the Father, full of grace and truth. John 1:14

Jesus was not just another man who happened to be crucified. He was the Son of God, pure gold, yet He presented Himself to die on our behalf. The fact that He died for our sins and also that He rose again from the dead are reflected in the images of the Lampstand. Even then, thousands of years before Jesus was born, God was already indicating that the One who would be smitten would rise again.

The Lampstand had seven branches, each with its separate flame, and seven is the number of perfection, or completeness. So the Lampstand, again, is the symbol of Jesus Christ because He is and was perfect and complete:

> *For in him dwelleth all the fulness of the Godhead bodily. And ye are complete in him, which is the head of all principality and power. Colossians 2:9-10, KJV*

The Lampstand was complete, and our Lord has given us, through the Perfect One, Jesus, all that we will ever need to be successful in life. Because He is full and complete, we are full and complete in Him.

The Lampstand was the only light or open flame in the Tabernacle, and without it the Tabernacle would have been completely dark at night. Without Jesus, this world we live in would be completely dark.

THE WHOLE WORLD LIES IN DARKNESS

This is a day of trouble and darkness, and all over the world there is distress. No area of life is void of confusion and sorrow. Seeds of discord are being sown everywhere. No one is safe, and no place is secure. War seems to be humanity's hobby, the game men love to play. The races seem to be drifting further apart, rather than coming closer together. Crime is persistent. The HIV/Aids pandemic is sweeping across the world, killing millions in its wake. Our world is indeed dark, dark because of sin.

The Bible considers every sinner to be in darkness. This is because he is morally blinded and fails to choose the right pathway. It is because he goes in the wrong direction and heads toward the wrong destination. Although he seeks joy and happiness, what he finds is sorrow and trouble.

He is in darkness because light can only come from God, and without God, there can only be darkness.

In Isaiah's day, men looked to idols for help and for light, and it is no different today. Men now look to education, science, power, wealth, and even pleasure for the secrets to life. Still, they dwell in darkness:

> *Then they will look to the earth, and see trouble and darkness, gloom of anguish, and they will be driven into darkness.* Isaiah 8:22

This is the sad plight of so many. We are more wealthy and have finer homes, finer automobiles, a finer education, and finer jobs than any previous generation, and yet the real joy of life seems to elude the great majority of people. Although they search for it, they never really find it.

Isaiah had the privilege of announcing to a darkened world the coming of Light:

> *The people who walked in darkness have seen a great light; those who dwelt in the land of the shadow of death, upon them a light has shined.* Isaiah 9:2

If anyone had a doubt about what exactly Isaiah was saying, he got more specific a few verses later:

> *For unto us a Child is born, unto us a son is given; and the government will be upon His shoulder. And His name will be called Wonderful, Counselor, Mighty God, Everlasting Father, Prince of Peace.* Isaiah 9:6

When Jesus came along, He said:

> *"I am the light of the world. He who follows me shall not walk in darkness, but have the light of life."* John 8:12

HOW IS JESUS THE LIGHT OF THE WORLD?

Jesus is the Light of the World because He activates the soul of man. Light is the essential condition of sight, and it is the action of light on the optic nerve that activates it and causes it to function. When light is absent, optic nerves tend to degenerate and devolve into uselessness. Light produces sight because it enters the pupil and is focused on the retina, and then the optic nerve transports the image produced to the brain. In the same way, there is a part of man that is inactive, it never lives, until it has been activated by the presence of Jesus. His light has the power to activate men's souls.

Man is never fully equipped or even fully alive unless and until He has the Light of the World focused on him. This is why Jesus could say:

I have come that they may have life, and that they may have it more abundantly. John 10:10

His light quickens us, gives us life:

And you hath he quickened, who were dead in trespasses and sins. Ephesians 2:1, KJV

Jesus can do this for us because His light is life-giving. When it touches us, our moral and spiritual capacities spring to life. He is the Light of the World because we only really live when He shines upon us.

Jesus is the Light of the World because He enables us to know what God is like. Before Jesus came, God seemed to be a strange, far-off deity who caused fear in the hearts of men. Before Jesus, God was considered to be a God of punishment, judgment, and death. But when the light went on, it illuminated the face of God and revealed Him for the first time as a God of love and compassion.

Jesus Himself declared:

For God so loved the world that He gave His only begotten Son, that whoever believes in Him should not perish but have everlasting life. John 3:16

Jesus is able to show us the face of God because He *is* God. One of His names is Emmanuel, and it literally means *"God with us"* (Matthew 1:23). He can show us God because He is God's Word to us.

God, who at various times and in various ways spoke in time past to the fathers by the prophets, has in these last days spoken to us by His Son. Hebrews 1:1-2

Jesus said very pointedly:

He who has seen Me has seen the Father. John 14:9

If you want to see God, you must go through Jesus Christ, His Son.

Jesus is the Light of the World because He throws the light on sin and evil. Men no longer have the cover of darkness. He said:

And this is the condemnation, that the light has come into the world, and men loved darkness rather than light, because their deeds were evil. For everyone practicing evil hates the light and does not come to the light, lest his deeds should be exposed. But he who does the truth comes to the light, that his deeds may be clearly seen, that they have been done in God. John 3:19-21

If you are one of those who are trying to get as far away from God as possible and still be *in* God, it must be because there are aspects of your character that love darkness. If, on the other hand, you're trying to get as close to God as you can, it is a clear signal that you love the light. You welcome the floodlight of heaven to shine on your soul, and you are more than willing for anything that should not be there to be revealed so that it can be removed.

If this is true, you have no problem praying, "Search me, O God. Search my mind. Search my heart, my will, my whole life, and if You find anything that should not be there, remove it as only You can."

Jesus is the Light of the World because His light enables us to see ourselves. That's hard for us to do, but we can when He turns the light of God on us. The year that King Uzziah died, Isaiah went into the house of God depressed and burdened. Everything was falling apart, and he was upset about all that was happening around him. Then he saw the Lord. He was *"high and lifted up,"* and *"His robe filled the temple"* (Isaiah

6:1). He saw the seraphim flying to and fro crying out:

> *"Holy, holy, holy is the Lord of hosts; the whole earth is full of His glory!"*
> Isaiah 6:3

There, in the light of God's glory, the prophet stopped thinking and talking about King Uzziah and his death, about his enemies and how they were doing him wrong, and about the difficult circumstances surrounding his life. Suddenly his vision focused on himself, and he cried out:

> *"Woe is me, for I am undone! Because I am a man of unclean lips, and I dwell in the midst of a people of unclean lips."* Isaiah 6:5

When Isaiah saw God and His glory, he could suddenly see himself as he really was.

We don't have time to get caught up in other people's business and to talk about who's doing what. We have too much work to do for God, and we're too busy trying to work on our own faults and needs. If you are busy looking around at everyone else, it may be because you have not yet focused on the Light of the World. See Him as you need to see Him, and you'll lose interest in the latest gossip and get busy preparing yourself for eternity.

Jesus is the Light of the world because if we allow Him to do it, His light and fire will consume sin in us. When Isaiah cried out, *"Woe is me ...because I am a man of unclean lips,"* his sin was nothing that God couldn't handle. God knew exactly what to do about it. He sent an angel to the altar, where he picked up a hot coal of fire, took it back, and placed it upon the lips of the prophet. Then he said:

> *"Behold, this has touched your lips; your iniquity is taken away, and your sin purged."* Isaiah 6:6

> *Jesus is the Light of the World because His light enables us to see ourselves.*

Suddenly, Isaiah was ready to do God's bidding. He responded:

"Here am I! Send me." Isaiah 6:8

When God's light gets through cleaning you up, then you'll be ready to do something serious for Him.

Jesus is the Light of the World because He lets us see what's real and what's false. For too long now we have chased after hallucinations and dreams, clinging to the artificial, hoping to find fulfillment. But it can't be found at Nieman Marcus, at the exercise spa, or in John or Josephine. It can only be found in the Almighty God of the Universe.

The light of God shows us what's transitory and phony, and when you really look with the light of God, you can easily see what will pass away. The Lord Jesus tells us:

Do not lay up for yourselves treasures on earth, where moth and rust destroy and where thieves break in and steal; but lay up for yourselves treasures in heaven, where neither moth nor rust destroys and where thieves do not break in and steal. Matthew 6:19-20

A moth flew in our front door one day not long ago, and my dear wife was quite upset about it. "Catch that moth," she cried. She knew how much damage a moth could do. Moths are going to be around for a very long time, and rust will be around as long as we live, but if we can store up our treasures somewhere that these elements don't harm them, they will be safe. Heaven is just such a place.

Later, Isaiah asked the question:

Why do you spend money for what is not bread, and your wages for what does not satisfy? Listen carefully to Me, and eat what is good, and let your soul delight itself in abundance. Incline your ear, and come to Me. Hear, and your soul shall live; and I will make an everlasting covenant with you—the sure mercies of David. Isaiah 55:2-3

Jesus is the true Bread of Life. Eat of Him.

In the light of Jesus we learn that the world with all of its treasures will one day pass away. In the light of Jesus we learn that grass will wither and flowers will fade, but the Word of our God will endure forever. In the light of Jesus we learn that He never changes. He is *"the Alpha,"* the beginning, and He is *"the Omega,"* the ending (Revelation 1:8). So when you've tried everything and everything has failed, it's time to try Jesus.

Your heart is longing for something real. You're tired of the phony, of cheap imitations, and you want the real thing. Jesus alone can satisfy. He alone is what your heart really needs. He is the only Light of the World.

Jesus is the Light of the World because He shows us the best pathway through life. There are many pitfalls along the way and many detours, and therefore it is often difficult for us to find our way. David refused to depend upon himself. Rather he prayed:

Oh, send out Your light and Your truth! Let them lead me; let them bring me to Your holy hill and to Your tabernacle. Psalm 43:3

Although David was quite young, he knew what would lighten his pathway.

Jesus said that He was *"the light of life"* (John 8:12), and this is why a previous generation sang that beloved hymn written by Bernard Barton (1784-1849) in 1826:

Walk in the light, beautiful light.
Come where the dewdrops of mercy shine bright.
Shine all around us by day and by night.

Oh, yes, Jesus is the Light of the World.

Jesus is the Light of the World because He brightens every situation. There is no situation so dark that He can not brighten it. It can never be dark as long as He is involved. David sang confidently:

Yea, though I walk through the valley of the shadow of death, I will fear no evil; for You are with me; Your rod and Your staff, they comfort me. Psalm 23:4

Even when I am not feeling well physically, it is a joy to know that I am not alone. The Good Shepherd is with me, and as long as He is there, my world can never be darkened.

Fall down before the Lord Jesus, and He will light your fire.

❀

As Christians, we have something on the inside that spurs us on. We don't get the blues like others do because Jesus, the Author and Finisher of our faith, is on our side. And in every situation, I'm grateful that I have Him in my life.

We may not always have money, we may not always have friends, and we may not be as highly educated as others, but we can be grateful that the Lord is with us. *"[His] rod and [His] staff, they comfort [us]."* As the songwriter C. Austin Miles (1868-1946) has written about 1908:

> *If Jesus goes with me, I'll go anywhere.*
> *'Tis heaven to me where'er I may be if He is there.*

You might live in the worst part of town, but if He's there, it's all right. You might have holes in your pockets and holes in your shoes, but if He's there, it's all right.

Jesus is the Light of the World because He will always share with us His quality of light. As we have seen, the children of Israel were told not to light a fire in the Tabernacle from any other flame but from the fire that God had sent. That fire must be taken to the Candlestick. That fire must be taken to the Altar of Incense. And if you have Jesus in your life, you won't need any other fire. You won't need to run here and there. Fall down before the Lord Jesus, and He will light your fire. He will turn you on.

You don't need any more coke or speed or grass. Turn on with Jesus. He loves to turn things on, and He's ready to turn you on too.

When He was lying in the manger as a newborn babe, He reached up and touched the star and turned it on. Later, during His ministry, He went by Lazarus' tomb, called him to come forth, and turned him on.

Eventually, He went back to the Father, but He sent the Comforter in His place. When the Spirit came into the world, He came as fire, sitting upon each of the believers and turning them on:

And they were all filled with the Holy Spirit and began to speak with other tongues, as the Spirit gave them utterance. Acts 2:4

John the Baptist had prophesied:

I indeed baptize you with water; but One mightier than I is coming, whose sandal strap I am not worthy to loose. He will baptize you with the Holy Spirit and fire. Luke 3:16

The Spirit's fire will turn you on too.

Aren't you glad that you know Jesus? If you know Him, you can become *"a new creature"* (2 Corinthians 5:17, KJV). When Jesus, the Light of the World, turns you on, He'll give you a new way of walking, a new way of talking, a new way of living and a new way of loving. He'll take you higher than you've ever been before.

THE LAMPSTAND REPRESENTS US

Just as the Lampstand was the light of the Tabernacle, Jesus is the Light of the World, but He went back to the Father in heaven. That is why He called together His disciples and said to them:

You are the light of the world. A city that is set on a hill cannot be hidden. Nor do they light a lamp and put it under a basket, but on a lampstand, and it gives light to all who are in the house. Let your light so shine before men, that they may see your good works and glorify your Father in heaven. Matthew 5:14-16

Today, our Lord Jesus says to us. "I have shared with you My quality of life. I have turned you on. Now you burn with the same fire that

I burn with. Now it's up to you to be the light of the world, to turn the world on to Me.

"Wherever you go, tell men and women about Me. Wherever you go, shine for Me. Wherever you go, light the way. Wherever you go, turn men and women on to My righteousness.

"Tell the good news over the backyard fence. Tell it in the barbershop and the beauty salon. Tell it while you're working on your job. Everywhere you go, tell it. I've given you My light; now go and spread that light."

You've never seen as clearly as you do now with Jesus in your life, and so He can guide you around the messes of life (and out of the messes of life), He can lead you around every pitfall and take you in the way of righteousness and joy, and He can make you a blessing to others around you.

I'm so glad I know Him and that I'm now living on the bright side.

Every time you go to the house of the Lord, ask Him to refresh your fire and to brighten your light, revive your soul, and reanimate your spirit, so that you can be the light of the world, as He needs you to be.

You're getting closer to the realm of divine encounter. Just take a couple more very important steps, and you'll be there.

Chapter Seven

THE ALTAR OF INCENSE
PRAYER AND WORSHIP

You shall make an altar to burn incense on; you shall make it of acacia wood.

And you shall overlay its top, its sides all around, and its horns with pure gold; and you shall make for it a molding of gold all around.

And you shall put it before the veil that is before the ark of the Testimony, before the mercy seat that is over the Testimony, where I will meet with you. Aaron shall burn on it incense every morning; when he tends the lamps, he shall burn incense on it. And when Aaron lights the lamps at twilight, he shall burn incense on it, a perpetual incense before the Lord throughout your generations. Exodus 30:1, 3, and 6-8

And the Lord said to Moses: "Take sweet spices, stacte and onycha and galbanum, and pure frankincense with these sweet spices; there shall be equal amounts of each. You shall make of these an incense, a compound according to the art of the perfumer, salted, pure, and holy. And you shall beat some of it very fine, and put some of it before the Testimony in the tabernacle of meeting where I will meet with you. It shall be most holy to you. But as for the incense which you shall make, you shall not make any for yourselves, according to its composition. It shall be to you holy for the Lord. Whoever makes any like it, to smell it, he shall be cut off from his people." Exodus 30:34-38

We are ready to take another step toward divine encounter. Get ready for it, for this is an important one.

This altar, called the Altar of Incense, or the Golden Altar, was the fifth item of furniture to be seen upon entering the Tabernacle. It was located just outside the Most Holy Place, or Holy of Holies, in front of the Veil. As the name implies, incense was burned on the altar. The burning of incense was done then, as it is now, to spread a sweet fragrance throughout the area, but it also had a far greater significance.

As a perfume, the burning incense did serve a very practical purpose. Foul smells were pervasive and inescapable in the ancient world. Think of a world where there were no underground sewers, where men and animals occupied the same living spaces, where each family slaughtered and dressed its own meat, poultry, and fish, and where there were no refrigerators or freezers. Think of a world where water and bathtubs were scarce, and where there was no soap as we know it today. Think of a world where there were no washing machines, no laundry detergent, no dryers, no laundries, and no dry cleaners. Think of a world where there was no mouthwash, shampoo, or toothpaste, no toilet paper, no disposable pads, no tissue, no deodorants or air fresheners, no garbage disposals, and no garbage collection trucks. There were also no undertakers (as we know them), and few could afford embalming. How could you escape foul smells in such a world?

Even the Court of the Tabernacle itself could not avoid the stench of the animals which were constantly sacrificed there. Their odor joined with the smell of the blood which the priests carried into the Tabernacle to cause offense to both God and man, for both have a constitutional dislike for foul odors and an affection for and an attraction to pleasant ones.

LEAVING A PLEASANT ODOR

Much of the animal kingdom has a very keen sense of smell. Odors, for many animals, not only attract or repel; they also provide identification and even communication. An odor also says something about us humans. As we begin to relate to each other, we work to eliminate foul odors and to project attractive odors as a sign of respect for those around us.

Each of us has preferences when it comes to smells. Frequently we give others fragrances that we like ourselves, rather than inquiring about what is pleasant to them. What smells good to one does not always smell as good to another.

But leaving in our wake a bad odor is so offensive that we have created phrases like *stinking* and *foul* to describe other things that we don't like, aside from physical smells: a stinking personality, for instance, or a foul attitude. Some people seem to have a stinky character. Some create an offensive emotional or mental atmosphere that seems to linger and be just as annoying as any bad smell. A stink is clearly not something we like, and if a person stinks—physically or in some other way—we find that person repugnant.

We create bad odors like these in many ways—by filling the atmosphere with negative words and thoughts and inconsiderate actions and attitudes, by imposing something upon others against their will, or by pushing upon them our own desires and agenda. Conversely, we can create a pleasant, sweet-smelling atmosphere around us—by learning to smile more and to really listen to others, by not complaining and criticizing, by loving people, affirming and complementing them, and always having something good to say about them.

When we encourage those around us, it changes the atmosphere. It is hard enough to make it through life as it is without having some negative person polluting your atmosphere so that you can hardly breathe.

Therefore, each of us must make an effort to become a sweet fragrance, a breath of fresh air, to others around us. Every room we step into should benefit from our positive, considerate, outreaching kindness.

Ask yourself how you can make the experience others have with you more pleasant and enjoyable, and then behave accordingly. Make more of an effort to assure that others enjoy being around you. There's nothing wrong with that, and by doing so, you spread a good aroma everywhere you go.

AROMAS THAT ARE PLEASING TO GOD

The Old Testament mentions at least two aromas that were pleasing to God. One of them I have difficulty understanding. It is found in Exodus 29:18:

> And you shall burn the whole ram on the altar. It is a burnt offering to the Lord; it is a sweet aroma [a sweet savour, KJV], an offering made by fire to the Lord.

The phrase "a sweet aroma [savour]" occurs in reference to burnt offerings forty-three times in the Old Testament. The thing that I have never been able to understand is that the sacrifices were burned with their skin and hair and even their entrails. But anyone who has ever been to a beauty salon knows that burning hair does not smell good at all. So, when the hair, skin, organs and entrails of animals were burned on the altar, most people would not have considered it to be a sweet-smelling aroma. So, why did God consider it to be pleasant?

It was because the smell of the sacrifice meant that the people of God were repenting and offering up sacrifices as an atonement for their sins. It meant that because of the shedding of blood, God could remit their sins. It meant that because of the sacrifice on the Brazen Altar, the priest could go into the Holy Place and the High Priest into the Most Holy Place. So it was a sweet fragrance to God, not because He enjoyed the smell of burning flesh and hair, but because the smell of rising smoke from the altar meant that the door to forgiveness was open to His people.

Sometimes a bad smell can be good. Let me explain what I mean by that. One very elderly gentleman, when his wife passed away, married a young woman. Because she was so young, a friend of his questioned his judgment. "Why did you choose such a young woman?" he asked. "Isn't she too young for you?"

"Maybe," the old man answered, "but I'd rather smell perfume than liniment any day of the week."

What the man didn't realize was this: maybe his young wife would need only perfume, but when the pain of arthritis or rheumatism eventually attacked him, he would be glad to smell some liniment on his own body. Bad-smelling liniment can smell pretty good when it is relieving terrible pain in your joints. Young people may laugh at that, but their day is coming.

When Jesus died on the cross for the sins of the world, His terrible sacrifice was an acceptable and sweet-smelling aroma to God:

Yet it pleased the Lord to bruise Him; He has put Him to grief. When You make His soul an offering for sin, He shall see His seed, He shall prolong His days, and the pleasure of the Lord shall prosper in His hand. He shall see the labor of His soul, and be satisfied. By His knowledge My righteous Servant shall justify many, for He shall bear their iniquities. Isaiah 53:10-11

In this case, again, a bad aroma became a good one.

The other aroma that was pleasing to God was the incense burning on the Golden Altar. It not only filled the Tabernacle with a sweet-smelling aroma; it was symbolic of the prayers, praises, and worship of the children of God.

The Bible often associates worship and prayer with the burning of incense:

Let my prayer be set before You as incense, the lifting up of my hands as the evening sacrifice. Psalm 141:2

ENCOUNTERING GOD

Child of God, when you are praying before Him, a sweet aroma is being sent up to His presence, and this is pleasing to Him. When you lift up your hands to Him, it is like *the evening sacrifice,* and this, again, is pleasing to Him:

I will offer to You the sacrifice of thanksgiving, and will call upon the name of the Lord. Psalm 116:17

Now when He had taken the scroll, the four living creatures and the twenty-four elders fell down before the Lamb, each having a harp, and golden bowls full of incense, which are the prayers of the saints. Revelation 5:8

Then another angel, having a golden censer, came and stood at the altar. And he was given much incense, that he should offer it with the prayers of all the saints upon the golden altar which was before the throne. And the smoke of the incense, with the prayers of the saints, ascended before God from the angel's hand. Revelation 8:3-4

When you pray, you are coming before the Lord with a golden bowl of flaming incense. And when you worship you are giving Him *"the sacrifice of praise"*:

Therefore by Him let us continually offer the sacrifice of praise to God, that is, the fruit of our lips, giving thanks to His name. Hebrews 13:15

No wonder God is pleased! Solomon wrote:

The prayer of the upright is His delight. Proverbs 15:8

To me, as with most parents, it is a source of joy when my children come to talk with me. They may have nothing particular in mind to discuss; they just want to talk. I love it, and our heavenly Father feels the very same way about us coming to Him. Our prayers and our worship reach out to Him and ascend before Him as a sweet-smelling sacrifice.

The Golden Altar was separated from the Holy of Holies and the Ark of the Covenant in it by a curtain (or veil), but the smoke from the Altar would surely find its way through tiny cracks into the Holy of Holies, and thus the prayers of the saints would come before the throne of God. But when Jesus died on the cross, the Veil was torn in two, and our prayers now have free access to the throne of God.

It may seem like your prayers are not going through, but the opened veil lets you know that the Lord will indeed hear you, and He *will* answer your prayers. And your praises are so pleasing to God that He actually takes up residence in them:

> *When God's people praise Him, not only are they reaching out to Him, but He is reaching out to them.*
>
> ❧

But You are holy, enthroned in the praises of Israel. Psalm 22:3

When God's people praise Him, not only are they reaching out to Him, but He is reaching out to them. He then comes down and sets His throne among us. As we saw in Chapter 4, this results in many varied blessings for us.

TRUE WORSHIP

The worship of the people of Israel came only after sacrifice and forgiveness at the Brazen Altar, cleansing at the Bronze Laver, consecration and fellowship at the Table of Showbread, and enlightenment through God and His Word at the Golden Lampstand. Real New Testament worship has its foundations in all of these things.

There is clearly a true worship and a false, or superficial one, and there are, therefore, true worshipers and superficial worshipers. Jesus said to the Samaritan woman:

But the hour is coming, and now is, when the true worshipers will worship the Father in spirit and truth; for the Father is seeking such to worship Him. God is Spirit, and those who worship Him must worship in spirit and truth. John 4:23-24

If we have not come to know Jesus as our sacrificial Lamb, how can we worship Him effectively? If we have not been cleansed at the Laver, how can we worship effectively? If we have not become the bread on the Table, experiencing fellowship with God and man, how can we worship effectively? If we have not been enlightened though the light of God and His Word, how can we worship Him effectively? These are all prerequisites to real worship.

Real worship is also fervent, fiery. As the incense was placed on a flaming altar and the flames of the altar ignited it, you also need some fire in your praise and worship and in your prayers. James wrote of the power of a *"fervent"* prayer:

The effective, fervent prayer of a righteous man avails much. James 5:16

These words *effective* and *fervent* come from the Greek word *energeo*, from which we get out word *energy*. Effective and fervent prayers are hot. That lets me know that it's all right to put some energy into your prayer, your praise, and your worship. Personally, I'm tired of the cold, abstract, and aloof prayers that some people offer up to God, and I can't stand a cold, dry worship. If you are one of those who say, "I'll let others get excited," then I'm afraid that you're prayer won't accomplish very much. It is the energetic prayer, the *"fervent prayer"* that touches the heart of God and *"avails much."* And the same is true of our worship. It should always be enthusiastic.

Worship is also consuming. When the incense was burned, its identity changed. And when you begin to worship in truth, you will be changed too. True and fervent worship will change even the look on your face, like it did the face of Moses. When he came back from being in the presence of the Lord, his face was shining.

True and fervent worship will change your walk and your talk. You can't go into the presence of the Lord and come out the same. True and fervent worship will consume you:

> He who finds his life will lose it, and he who loses his life for My sake will find it.
> Matthew 10:39

If you really want to live, lose yourself in worship to God.

If you really want to live, lose yourself in worship to God. If you want to be truly blessed, learn to praise Him. As you praise Him, your faith is lifted to a new level, and you suddenly know that you can make it. You can go through whatever you are facing when you praise God faithfully, and you always come out higher than you were before.

You may be bereaved and heartbroken, you may be in economic difficulty and not know how to come out of it, and your loved ones may have turned their backs and walked away from you, but God is still alive. If you will praise Him, He will put a smile on your face, and running in your feet. If you will praise Him, the blessings of the Lord will overflow in your life.

Real worship will fill the room with a fragrance pleasing to God, and it will also fill your life with a fragrance that will be pleasing to others.

THE PERFUME OF THE PRIESTS

As we have seen, it is a pleasure to be in the presence of some people. They are clean, not just sprayed with strong perfume. When people are unclean, perfume only makes things worse. Taking a bath prepares you to put on a perfume that is pleasant.

The anointing oil was the perfume of the priests, but before they could put it on, they had to go back to the Laver. When you are clean and the anointing of the Lord has rested upon you, you, too, will give off a pleasant aroma to those around you.

The anointing oil, with its special mixture of elements, and the holy incense, which was unique among all incenses, were special to God and man. There was nothing quite like them in all the earth. These substances were so holy that God warned the people not to try to duplicate them and use them for other purposes. If they did, the penalty was death.

This was serious. God wanted something from the people that no one else was getting. He wanted them to give to Him something they gave to no one else. In the same way, God wants our special praise and worship. If you get more excited about anyone or anything else than you do about God, then He's not happy with that. He wants your highest praise, and He wants your highest commitment. If you are more involved with and committed to anything other than God, He is upset about that fact. There is nothing inherently wrong with attending sporting and musical events, but if we are willing to do in those venues what we are not willing to do for God inside (or outside) of His house, He is angry about it. Child of God, do more for God than you do for anything or anyone else, and then He'll know that you love Him.

Clap your hands! Move your feet! Do something to let God know that you are praising Him, that you love Him, that you're going to magnify and glorify His name. Jesus taught:

Seek ye first the kingdom of God, and his righteousness; and all these things shall be added unto you. Matthew 6:33

In other words, you can praise your way into your blessing. You can love your way into your prosperity. You can worship your way into your healing. When you let God know that He's first, then He'll pour out upon you the blessing you need. But He is jealous, and He has to be first.

Some sit in church with crossed arms and legs and then when they're out on the street, they turn the radio to some rock station and start diddly-bopping down the street. But if you're not willing to do it for God, then don't do it for others. If, in the street, you're bobbing your head and moving your feet, then give God something more when it comes time to praise Him. If you are the life of the party when you gather with your friends (the first one there and the last to leave) but in church, you sit in silence, you're not pleasing to God. Get out in the aisle of your church, raise your hands to God, and start praising Him.

You may feel that you don't know what to say to God, but that's not an acceptable excuse. If you know what to say to others, why is it that you don't know what to say to God? Try this:

Lord,

Everything that I have You gave to me, and everything that I am You made me. Everything I know You taught me. Nobody's blessed me like You have blessed me. And so I will bless You today.

David was just a lad, but he sang out:

Bless the Lord, O my soul; and all that is within me, bless His holy name! Bless the Lord, O my soul, and forget not all His benefits: Who forgives all your iniquities, Who heals all your diseases, Who redeems your life from destruction, Who crowns you with lovingkindness and tender mercies, Who satisfies your mouth with good things, so that your youth is renewed like the eagle's. Psalm 103:1-5

Yes, bless His holy name.

God has been so good to you, therefore you need to praise Him. How can you *not* praise Him? (More will be said on this subject of offering God the highest praise in the next chapter.)

When we praise God, He shows up, and when He shows up, anything is possible. Praise, therefore, brings deliverance. It brings healing. It brings blessing. And it brings you closer to God and to the realm of the miraculous.

This Altar of Incense was nearer to the Holy of Holies than any other item of furniture in the Holy Place, and as we learn to praise God, we're getting closer to Him too. We are advancing toward His glory. Nothing could be more important than the praise of God, the honor of God, the glory of God. It is this experience that carries you right up to the door of the Most Holy Place, right up to the entrance into God's very best for your life. Bring your sacrifice of praise, and come before Him.

AVOIDING *"STRANGE FIRE"*?

In the previous chapter, while laying the foundation for light and fire, I explored the establishment of God's holy fire upon the altar of the Tabernacle. What I didn't say there was that not everyone respected the holy fire He had given, and not everyone obeyed His commands concerning it. As a result, two men died.

They were Nadab and Abihu, two of Aaron's sons, and they had been consecrated to the priesthood. Seeing the miracles that were happening, these two young men were suddenly filled with pride and enthusiasm for their newly-obtained responsibilities and privileges, and this caused them to go beyond what God had authorized or commanded them to do. They felt that they, too, should be performing some special religious duty—as Moses and Aaron were—so they took it upon themselves to do so.

It should be remembered that every action or ritual had been ordained by God and passed on to the priests by Moses, and Moses had been very careful to see that everything was done exactly as God had commanded. He neither added to nor took away from God's words. We are all admonished in scripture to do the same.

Nadab and Abihu were not nearly as cautious as their Uncle Moses. Without being told to do so by God (or by Moses or Aaron) they went before the altar to offer incense. In their rush to do *something*, they ignored and disregarded and bypassed the fire which God had sent from heaven and did not use this fire to ignite their own fire. Rather, they used fire of unknown origin, which the Bible then calls *"profane fire."* The result was disastrous:

> *Then Nadab and Abihu, the sons of Aaron, each took his censer and put fire in it, put incense on it, and offered profane fire before the*

Lord, which He had not commanded them. So fire went out from the Lord and devoured them, and they died before the Lord. Leviticus 10:1-2

The King James Version of the Bible calls this fire *"strange fire."* It was *"strange"* because it was not the fire God had ordained, and the action of these two men caused God's wrath to fall on them. Fire had fallen from heaven before, and now it came again, but this time, it was for their destruction.

It was a serious error for these men to do anything without instructions from, or at the very least, the approval of God or from Moses, His servant. Since God through Moses had made them priests, they should have respected Moses' leadership more. New responsibilities or anointings should never be the cause for one to disrespect leadership. You may have the anointing and the power, but no matter how much anointing and power you have, there are still some aspects of your life that require you to remain under subjection to a more mature person.

Also, an anointing and the presence of God's power in your life, and with them, the attainment of some position, should never cause you to feel that *anything* you do will be acceptable to God. As powerful as you might be, you still have to do things God's way.

The zeal of these two men was *"not according to knowledge"* (Romans 10:2), for only one priest was ordered to offer incense at a time, never two. Nadab and Abihu were like many who do not seek God's will or the word of God's leader and frequently find themselves doing the exact opposite of what God would have them to do. It is possible to be filled with the Spirit and speak in tongues and still get on a wrong road.

Nadab and Abihu disregarded what God had provided for them and substituted something else in its place. Why would they need a fire from some other source when God had already sent down an ever-burning fire? What could possibly be better than what God had provided? Their error proved fatal.

To some, it might seem that the punishment of Nadab and Abihu was too severe, but we must remember that they expressed contempt for God, for Moses, for God's will, His law, and His holiness, and that could not be overlooked. A proper relationship with God produces the proper order in your life, and when your relationship with God is not right, that fact will be manifested in your behavior.

Careless and improper worship of God implies a careless and improper relationship with Him, and this is dangerous.

What does all of this have to do with worship? Careless and improper worship of God implies a careless and improper relationship with Him, and this is dangerous. The severe punishment of Nabab and Abihu was a warning to others (and to us) that those who worship before God must not only sanctify themselves; they must also consider God and His service to be most holy. They should never approach God's altar lightly, without awe and reverence in their hearts. If you want to be blessed, you can't come in your own way. You have to come in God's way. If you disrespect God's house, His presence, and His servants, what can you expect from God but judgment?

In the time of the early church, a similar thing happened. The Church was born with a burst of God's fire:

When the Day of Pentecost had fully come, they were all with one accord in one place. And suddenly there came a sound from heaven, as of a rushing mighty wind, and it filled the whole house where they were sitting. Then there appeared to them divided tongues, as of fire, and one sat upon each of them. And they were all filled with the Holy Spirit and began to speak with other tongues, as the Spirit gave them utterance. Acts 2:1-4

John the Baptist had prophesied the coming of the fire:

John answered, saying to all, "I indeed baptize you with water; but One mightier than I is coming, whose sandal strap I am not worthy to loose, He will baptize you with the Holy Spirit and fire." Luke 3:16

It happened just as he had foretold. Just as fire from the Lord came early in the dispensation of the Law, so Pentecostal fire came early in the dispensation of grace. Just as Moses sent the priests into the Tabernacle for seven days of separation and consecration, Jesus sent the first believers into the Upper Room for ten days of consecration and prayer. And just as Nadab and Abihu were slain for disregarding God's Spirit, Ananias and Sapphira were slain for lying to the Holy Ghost (see Acts 5). This showed that God was just as serious about New Testament worship as He was about worship under the Law.

Because fire signifies the presence of God, fire remains a symbol of His involvement in our private and public worship. Just as God, through Moses, ordered the children of Israel to keep the fire burning in the Tabernacle, so we are commanded to make every provision so that the activity of the Holy Ghost will be kept alive and that the Holy Ghost will direct, empower, and rule our worship today.

God is looking for worshippers, but not just any worshippers:

But the hour is coming, and now is, when the true worshipers will worship the Father in spirit and truth; for the Father is seeking such to worship Him. God is Spirit, and those who worship Him must worship in spirit and truth. John 4:23-24

Our Father longs for worshippers who are not satisfied with the form and ceremony of worship. He looks for someone whose soul has been ignited with fire from on high and who is willing to offer up that same fire in worship to almighty God. It is an unfortunate fact that many offer up to God *"strange fire," "profane fire,"* going into the house of the Lord with their hearts filled with pride, just as did Nadab and Abihu.

Pride will make you want to be seen, to be recognized. It will cause you to act selfishly. It will make you want people to see you rather than see God. If you have such an attitude, you are treading on dangerous territory. In worship, you are not just standing before men; you are standing before the God of the universe. The cattle on a thousand hills are His. All the silver and the gold are His. His foolishness is as far above your greatest wisdom as the heavens are above the earth. You may be able to impress people, but God is not easily impressed. He made you, and He knows you like no other. He has a way of exalting the humble and humbling the exalted:

Everyone who exalts himself will be humbled, and he who humbles himself will be exalted. Luke 18:14

God resists the proud but gives grace to the humble. James 4:6

What, then, should we do. The Scriptures teach us:

Therefore humble yourselves under the mighty hand of God, that He may exalt you in due time. 1 Peter 5:6

Nadab and Abihu had a haughtiness about them that could not be overlooked. They thought they were getting ready to show the people something, so God had to show them something.

WE OFFER *"STRANGE FIRE"* WHEN ...

We offer strange fire when we are self-righteous and arrogant before God. It may be that you get through your days without committing overt acts of sin, but (again) what about your sins of omission? You may not have robbed a bank, but did you help any poor people? Did you do anything for the hungry? Did you lift anyone who was down? Did you tell anyone about Jesus? No matter how righteous we may be, the Lord assures us that we are little more than *"unprofitable servants,"* and that our righteousness is *"like filthy rags"*:

When you have done all those things which you are commanded, say, "We are unprofitable servants. We have done what was our duty to do." Luke 17:10

But we are all like an unclean thing, and all our righteousnesses are like filthy rags. Isaiah 64:6

Stop thinking about how much better you are than others and start realizing that it is only because of His grace and mercy that you are even alive.

We offer strange fire when we are unprepared morally and spiritually to worship God, when we come to Him with sin in our lives for which we have not repented and for which we have not received forgiveness. It is unwise to play around at the Golden Candlestick or the Altar of Incense. Rather, we should remove ourselves and get quickly back to the Brazen Alar and the Laver so that we can be washed and prepared. Repent and be washed again, and then you are ready for worship in the Holy Place.

We offer strange fire when we come to worship having unresolved conflicts with fellow believers:

Therefore if you bring your gift to the altar, and there remember that your brother has something against you, leave your gift there before the altar, and go your way. First be reconciled to your brother, and then come and offer your gift. Matthew 5:23-24

We offer strange fire when we come to worship with our minds filled with everything *but* thoughts of God. It's amazing how many people allow their minds to be easily distracted. When I'm speaking with someone, I want them to look me in the eye, forget about everything else, and talk to *me*. If they have something more important to do, then I prefer to keep the conversation for some other more appropriate time. But I hate it when people pretend to be talking with you, and it is obvious that their interest is elsewhere.

In the same way, God wants our full attention in worship. We don't go to church to see someone else, but to meet with *Him*.

We offer strange fire when we are careless in worship—half singing, half preaching, half praying, chewing gum, talking, walking up and down the aisles, disregarding God's house, coming late, leaving early, failing to teach and control our children. What kind of fire are you offering up to the Lord?

We offer strange fire when we are inappropriate in our worship—fleshly and irreverent. The appeal of worship must not be to the flesh, but rather to the spirit, and the focus must be on the Holy Spirit. Jude wrote:

But you, beloved, building yourselves up on your most holy faith, praying in the Holy Spirit ... Jude 20

Paul wrote:

There is therefore now no condemnation to those who are in Christ Jesus, who do not walk according to the flesh, but according to the Spirit. Romans 8:1

Come into the presence of the Lord with sincere spiritual hunger. Jesus said:

Blessed are those who hunger and thirst for righteousness, for they shall be filled. Matthew 5:6

Sing in the Spirit, and pray in the Spirit, just as Paul the apostle did:

I will pray with the spirit, and I will also pray with the understanding. I will sing with the spirit, and I will also sing with the understanding. 1 Corinthians 14:15

Worship in the Spirit, for His might in you is the only thing that will enable you to overcome. He said:

This is the word of the Lord... : "Not by might nor by power, but by My Spirit." Zechariah 4:6

Away with self, and away with the flesh. Worship God in the Spirit. Don't just go through the motions; worship Him *in truth.*

Some people just want to show off; they don't want to worship God. Some don't care about the words of a song; they just want to hear the music. Some just want to use God and the church to do their own thing. Some show by the way they dress, the way they walk, and the way they look that they are offering strange fire.

Emotionalism without spirituality is strange fire. The Spirit will quicken your emotions, but emotionalism alone is not what God is about. What are you shouting about? What are you screaming about? If you don't know, then stop until you do. Noise is not spirituality, loud singing and fast clapping is not spirituality. Get the real thing.

We offer strange fire when we seek substitutes for the working of the Spirit. New fires and new movements are popping up all around us, but the Pentecostal fires are still burning. It's time to stop imitating the Spirit and to start being filled with the true Spirit.

Jeremiah knew the genuine fire of the Lord. He said:

I said, "I will not make mention of Him, nor speak anymore in His name." But His word was in my heart like a burning fire shut up in my bones; I was weary of holding it back, and I could not.
Jeremiah 20:9

Our worship must be energized and directed *by* the Spirit of God, and it must be focused *on* the Spirit of God. When we learn to worship God as He deserves to be worshiped, we have stepped onto miracle territory and put ourselves in a position to be blessed.

VARIOUS HEBREW WORDS FOR PRAISE

In His Word, God tells us what to do, verbally and physically, when we praise and worship Him in our spirits. And, if we truly love Him, we will honor His desires. There are at least seven different Hebrew words used for praise in the Bible, and they tell us how to praise the Lord:

Offer to God thanksgiving, and pay your vows to the Most High.
Psalm 50:14

The Hebrew word translated here as *thanksgiving* is *todah*, which means to lift the hands in a cuplike manner, as in giving or receiving a gift or a sacrifice. Sometimes we need to hold our hands up in this manner, signifying to God that if there is anything in our hands that shouldn't be there, He can take it out. By the same token, we are signifying to Him that anything new He has for us, we want to receive it. Our hands are open to God, and our open hands are a sign that our lives are open to Him as well. He can come in and take over anytime He wants to.

Lift your open hands before the Lord and begin to glorify Him and bless His holy name.

The next Hebrew word for praise is *yadah*:

Enter into His gates with thanksgiving, and into His courts with praise. Be thankful to Him, and bless His name. Psalm 100:4

The word translated *thankful* in this passage is *yadah*, which means to lift up the hands, to worship with extended hands. This time our hands are stretched upward, and it feels right and good to do this. It is a sign of recognition of the greatness of God and of our acceptance of His sovereignty over us.

If someone pulls a gun on you, your first and automatic reaction is to raise your hands in the air. This is a universal sign of surrender, one that is understood and recognized all over the world. It is an admission that the other person has the upper hand, is more powerful, and that there is no question about who is in charge. If we do this for men, we should raise our hands even higher for God.

Sometimes we feel like actually waving our hands and arms before the Lord. That's even better. Do whatever is necessary to give God the praise He so richly deserves.

The next Hebrew word to be considered is *halal:*

You who fear the Lord, praise Him! Psalm 22:23

Halal means to be clamorously foolish about your love, to be unrestrained with your praises. Give God some *halal.* He loves it when you do. At this point, you don't care what others think about you. If you can act foolish at sporting events, you can do it for God too. Whatever you do for worldly events, do even more for God.

The next Hebrew word for praise is *shabach*:

Because Your lovingkindness is better than life, my lips shall praise You. Psalm 63:3

Shabach is a loud shout proclaiming the glory of God. This isn't something we would do continuously, but we should do it every once in a while.

We love to clap our hands, but the problem is that we do it for everyone. Once in a while, we need to do it just for the Lord. We get so happy sometimes that we dance a little. Do it for the Lord. Some of us are lavish with our praise of people. We should do that for the Lord. And sometimes something strikes us as so wonderful that we give out a joyous shout. Why can't we all do that for the Lord occasionally? He loves it, and He will bless you for it.

Some people try to act so sophisticated that the very thought of raising their voices and acting in an exuberant manner seems very out of character for them. But something excites you. Why not let it be the goodness of the Lord?

In church, some people seem to be always so reserved and controlled and even-tempered, but when they're not in church, they are sometimes very different. That's not right. God deserves your very best praise.

Maybe you don't feel like being demonstrative with your praise, and you want to praise the Lord in your own way. But that's unacceptable to God. He sets the standards when it comes to worship. He knows what He likes, and that's what He requires of us. Praise is for Him, and He has the right to have it like He wants it. If He wants exuberance, then only exuberance will do.

The next Hebrew word for praise is *zamar*:

Sing praise to the Lord, you saints of His, and give thanks at the remembrance of His holy name. Psalm 30:4

Zamar implies the use of musical instruments to praise the Lord. Lifting up your voice is wonderful, but the Lord wants more. Let your voice be accompanied by the sounds of various musical instruments. That's why we use many instruments in our public worship these days—the more the better.

The next Hebrew word for praise is *barak:*

I will bless the Lord at all times; His praise shall continually be in my mouth. Psalm 34:1

Barak means to kneel or bow, to rock back and forth, or from side to side. When the Spirit is present, many of God's people don't have to say anything at all, but their bodies are moving. They are swaying. Their heads are moving from side to side. They are feeling the presence of God.

We often react in a similar way to the sound of music or to something that is said to us. Why, then, can't we do it for the Lord? Let your body respond to God.

The final Hebrew word for praise that I want to consider here is *tehillah:*

But You are holy, enthroned in the praises of Israel. Psalm 22:3

Tehillah means to sing from your spirit, to glorify God in song, a song of spontaneous praise. This is very biblical:

Speaking to one another in psalms and hymns and spiritual songs, singing and making melody in your heart to the Lord, giving thanks always for all things to God the Father in the name of our Lord Jesus Christ. Ephesians 5:19-20

This is just singing out of your heart. It's not a song you have learned or practiced. It is spontaneous, new, fresh, and direct from your spirit to the heart of God. It gives God a throne to sit on, and He takes up residence in such praises.

What is the lesson from all of this? We need to be open to praise God in the way that the Spirit deems best. Sometimes we jump or run.

Sometimes we sing and shout. Sometimes our worship is organized, that is, we do it all together, and sometimes we do it individually. But praise God in the way He deserves to be praised. He is waiting to hear from YOU.

GOD IS WAITING TO HEAR FROM YOU

The singing of a church choir is wonderful, but God is waiting to hear YOUR voice. What a worship leader does may be wonderful, but God is waiting to hear from YOU: *"making melody in YOUR heart unto the Lord."* No other person can take your place when it comes to worshiping God.

We need to be open to praise God in the way that the Spirit deems best.

❧

You may not have a beautiful singing voice, and if that is true, others probably don't enjoy hearing you sing. But God loves to hear you sing to Him, and He's just waiting right now for you to lift up your voice.

Having praise in your heart and mind is not enough; you have to get physical and let it come out. How can you hold your peace? *"Let the redeemed of the Lord say so"*:

> *Let the redeemed of the Lord say so, whom He has redeemed from the hand of the enemy.* Psalm 107:2

You can't keep quiet any longer. You need to praise God.

GOD WILL GET PHYSICAL WITH YOU

If you can get physical with God, He will get physical with you. On the road to Emmaus, when two disciples had walked and talked with Jesus, they had not yet recognized Him, but they later said:

> *"Did not our heart burn within us, while He talked with us on the road?"* Luke 24:32

133

When you know God, He will place a burning down in your heart. When you know Him, you can feel His presence and His power. He physically manifests His presence in your life.

God got physical with those who loved Him on the Day of Pentecost:

When the Day of Pentecost had fully come, they were all with one accord in one place. And suddenly there came a sound from heaven, as of a rushing mighty wind, and it filled the whole house where they were sitting. Then there appeared to them divided tongues, as of fire, and one sat upon each of them. And they were all filled with the Holy Spirit and began to speak with other tongues, as the Spirit gave them utterance. Acts 2:1-4

The sound the disciples gathered in the Upper Room that day was real. It was an audible sound, and they all heard it. It was like a rushing wind, and it *"filled the whole house."*

Next, they saw something. It looked like tongues of fire, and it sat over each of them.

Then something even more strange happened. Those humble believers began speaking in foreign languages given to them miraculously by God. All of us should understand and appreciate this miraculous phenomenon.

When a group from our church accompanied me to the Ivory Coast (a French-speaking African nation) for ministry, some of us had to go to the police station one day to retrieve a camera temporarily confiscated from one of our members. As the leader of the group, I went forward and began speaking with the officer in charge regarding the camera. He acted as if he had not heard a word I said, and then he turned to the group and said in perfect English, "Is there anyone here who speaks French so that we may converse?" It was obvious that he spoke excellent English, but since French was his language, he wanted to speak French. He was the one in charge, and he was setting the acceptable language as

French, so since I couldn't speak French, I had to step aside and let somebody else do the talking that day.

On the Day of Pentecost, God gave His people other languages to praise Him in, and He is still doing that today. The key is that He gets to choose the language. In the moments He inspires you to speak another language, do it for His glory. It happened in Jerusalem on the Day of Pentecost, and it is still happening today in our modern world.

It's fine and wonderful to praise God in your own language, but when the Spirit urges you to praise Him in some other God-given words, words that you have not been taught and have never learned, respond to Him. He loves that. Jude wrote of this experience when he said:

But you, beloved, building yourselves up on your most holy faith, praying in the Holy Spirit ... Jude 20

There comes a time when all of the words we know won't express what our hearts feel. In that moment, the Spirit gives us other words to use. You will feel the urgency to speak out something you don't understand. Respond.

Speaking in tongues bypasses the understanding and frees us to express things we could not otherwise express, for we lack the vocabulary.

As we noted in a previous chapter, Paul also wrote of this experience:

For he who speaks in a tongue does not speak to men but to God, for no one understands him; however, in the spirit he speaks mysteries. 1 Corinthians 14:2

What is the conclusion then? I will pray with the spirit, and I will also pray with the understanding. I will sing with the spirit, and I will also sing with the understanding. 1 Corinthians 14:15

I am convinced that when I praise God in tongues the devil cannot know what I am saying and therefore cannot interfere. What I know for sure is that this experience takes me higher than I've ever been before.

After stating that praying in the Holy Spirit builds us up on our most holy faith, Jude concluded:

Now to Him who is able to keep you from stumbling, and to present you faultless before the presence of His glory with exceeding joy, to God our Savior, Who alone is wise, be glory and majesty, dominion and power, both now and forever. Amen. Jude 24-25

The more you praise God, the easier it will be for you to stand. He is able to keep you from falling and to present you faultless before the Father, so take time to worship Him. Draw near to Him through praise. Be strengthened through praise. Be energized through praise. Be changed through praise.

It's all right to raise your voice in praise. For if you don't praise God, someone else will. Don't miss your opportunity. I worry about people who never get excited about God. Something's wrong with their Christian experience. How can we *not* praise Him?

This is why God wants us to be involved with places and things and customs. When we do something in the physical, He becomes more real to us.

You were born to honor God, to give Him praise. You were born to worship Him. And if you haven't yet learned to do it, you are living below your privilege. It is time to worship Him *"in spirit and truth."*

BECOMING DEMONSTRATIVE

God became demonstrative in His love for us:

For when we were still without strength, in due time Christ died for the ungodly. For scarcely for a righteous man will one die; yet perhaps for a good man someone would even dare to die. But God demonstrates His own love toward us, in that while we were still sinners, Christ died for us. Romans 5:6-8

Jesus gave us a demonstration of His love for us, and every once in a while, we ought to give Him a demonstration of our love and devotion to Him. We need to get physical and allow our emotions to be acted out. If you feel something, let it be seen and known. If God is in your heart, let it show on the outside.

Wave your hands. Move your feet. Sing out His praises. Your emotions are not enough, and your words are not enough. Demonstrate your appreciation for Him.

Sometimes what we are feeling is difficult to express in words. Express it in actions. Wave your hands in the air. Stand up on your feet. Clap your hands to God. Let Him know that you appreciate the shedding of His blood on Calvary.

When you were in sin, He did something that could bring you out and turn you around. When you couldn't be good enough, He was good enough for you. When you couldn't be righteous enough, He was righteous enough for you. He has become your righteousness. He has become your grace. He has become your power to overcome sin. He is your help. He is your strength. He is worthy this day of all of our praises, for He has become Himself our substitutionary Lamb, and by the sacrifice of His own blood, we are saved. Now, that's something worth shouting about.

We are ready now to move on to that final step that will lead us into the presence of God.

Every step is an important one, accepting Jesus as our sacrificial Lamb, being cleansed by His blood, becoming the Bread upon God's altar and enjoying fellowship with Him and with our fellow believers, and learning to walk in the light of God and of His Word. But without true worship, none of these will make you the effective Christian God wants you to be.

When you have taken this all-important step, then, at last, you are ready to move on and possess what is rightfully yours. Press in now to experience your divine encounter.

Chapter Eight

THE ARK OF THE COVENANT

DIVINE ENCOUNTER

And they shall make an ark of acacia wood; two and a half cubits shall be its length, a cubit and a half its width, and a cubit and a half its height. And you shall overlay it with pure gold, inside and out you shall overlay it, and shall make on it a molding of gold all around.

You shall make a mercy seat of pure gold; two and a half cubits shall be its length and a cubit and a half its width.

You shall put the mercy seat on top of the ark, and in the ark you shall put the Testimony that I will give you. And there I will meet with you, and I will speak with you from above the mercy seat, from between the two cherubim which are on the ark of the Testimony, about everything which I will give you in commandment to the children of Israel. Exodus 25:10-11, 17 and 21-22

You have arrived at the place where God chooses to manifest His presence. To the children of Israel, having just escaped from slavery in Egypt, access to the presence of God in the Most Holy Place in their wilderness Tabernacle, or the Holy of Holies, as it was also known, was represented by a little wooden chest, or box, covered with gold. This box was called the Ark of the Covenant, or the Ark of the Testimony.

The Ark was not imposing in itself, measuring only about four feet long, two and a half feet wide, and two and a half feet high, but it was a beauty to behold. Like many of the furnishings of the Tabernacle, it was constructed of the durable, nearly imperishable, acacia wood. That was good in itself, but then it was overlaid within and without with sheets of pure gold.

On each side of the Ark were two rings designed so that a pole could be slipped into them. In this way, the Ark, much too sacred to be touched by human hands, could be carried without being contaminated. Everything about the Tabernacle was portable, because the children of Israel were on the move—on their way to the Promised Land.

On the lid of the Ark was a plate of pure gold that covered the chest completely. This plate was called the Mercy Seat. At each end of the Mercy Seat stood two golden angels facing one another, looking down on the Mercy Seat, and bowing. Their wings were stretched upward and forward so that they touched over the Mercy Seat.

THE SIGNIFICANCE OF THE ARK

For many reasons, the Ark of the Covenant, with its accompanying Mercy Seat, was the most important item of furniture in the Tabernacle. One of those reasons is that the Ark of the Covenant, it appears to me, is the only item of Tabernacle furniture that will be found in Heaven:

Then the temple of God was opened in heaven, and the ark of His covenant was seen in His temple. And there were lightnings, noises, thunderings, an earthquake, and great hail. Revelation 11:19

I don't understand exactly how the Ark of the Covenant will be there—whether materially or spiritually—but it *will* be there. And if God would retain that one piece of the Tabernacle furniture, then it must be very important.

The Ark was the first item of furniture God told Moses to build, and it was the first thing to be placed in the Tabernacle after it was constructed. It was to the Ark that all the other furnishings pointed.

The Ark occupied the most sacred area of the Tabernacle. As a matter of fact, the Tabernacle (and later, the Temple) were actually built to be a dwelling place *for* the Ark. This was a very important piece of furniture indeed. It was there, in this spot, that God chose to manifest His presence to Moses and thus to Israel.

When Moses needed to hear from God, he went into the Holy of Holies and communed with Him there.

THE CONTENTS OF THE ARK

The contents of the Ark were very significant:

Then Moses said, "This is the thing which the Lord has commanded: 'Fill an omer with it [manna], to be kept for your generations, that they may see the bread with which I fed you in the wilderness, when I brought you out of the land of Egypt." And Moses said to Aaron, "Take a pot and put an omer of manna in it, and lay it up before the Lord, to be kept for your generations." As the Lord commanded Moses, so Aaron laid it up before the Testimony, to be kept. Exodus 16:32-34

And the Lord said to Moses, "Bring Aaron's rod back before the Testimony, to be kept as a sign against the rebels, that you may put their complaints away from Me, lest they die." Numbers 17:10

And He wrote on the tablets according to the first writing, the Ten Commandments, which the Lord had spoken to you in the mountain from the midst of the fire in the day of the assembly; and the Lord gave them to me. Then I turned and came down from the mountain, and put the tablets in the ark which I had made; and there they are, just as the Lord commanded me. Deuteronomy 10:4-5

The writer of Hebrews summarized all of this:

And behind the second veil, the part of the tabernacle which is called the Holiest of All, which had the golden censer and the ark of the covenant overlaid on all sides with gold, in which were the golden pot that had the manna, Aaron's rod that budded, and the tablets of the covenant; and above it were the cherubim of glory overshadowing the mercy seat. Hebrews 9:3-5

Some have felt that 1 Kings 8:9 contradicts this, for it says, *"There was nothing in the ark except the two tablets of stone which Moses put there at Horeb, when the LORD made a covenant with the children of Israel, when they came out of the land of Egypt,"* but 1 Kings refers to a time several centuries later than that referred to in Hebrews. Hebrews refers to the actual Tabernacle, but 1 Kings refers to the Temple built by Solomon some centuries later. After some period of time, apparently the rod of Aaron and the pot of manna were removed, and only the tablets of stone remained.

Technically there were four items in the Ark, because there were two tablets of stone, but if we count the two tablets as one item, then there were only three. Each of these three items was the result of a miraculous occurrence, each was an expression of the love of God, each existed for the benefit of the people, and each referred to a past event which assured future blessings.

It is unfortunate and puzzling that each of these items came to be as a response by God to negative and disruptive behavior on the part of the people of Israel.

THE GOLDEN POT OF MANNA

In the first instance, they were caught complaining against God and the leadership He had appointed over them:

Then the whole congregation of the children of Israel complained against Moses and Aaron in the wilderness. And the children of Israel said to them, "Oh, that we had died by the hand of the Lord in the land of Egypt, when we sat by the pots of meat and when we ate bread to the full! For you have brought us out into this wilderness to kill this whole assembly with hunger." Exodus 16:2-3

God, working through Moses, had just brought these very people out of an ordeal of slavery and oppression that had lasted for many generations covering more than four hundred years. Moses had already been freed himself and was doing well in his personal life, but when God called him, he had agreed to return to Egypt to free his fellow Jews.

The Egyptians refused to allow the Hebrew slaves to go free, but God brought terrible plagues down upon them that ultimately forced the Pharaoh to let them go. Then God did many other wonderful miracles on behalf of His people. For instance, the Red Sea opened so that they could cross, and bitter, undrinkable water was made sweet so that they could drink. But that was just the beginning of many miracles they would receive at His hand. Still, after all of that, the people were found to be murmuring and complaining, and that is always a very serious offense against God.

On a personal level, murmuring, when it is directed at us, is not only offensive; it is also alienating. Even if we concede to a particular desire being expressed, we do so with a wounded spirit. Because of this, murmuring is counterproductive because it makes future favors much less likely. If we see someone coming who has recently wheedled a favor out of us by murmuring, we try to get out of their way as fast as we possibly can.

Murmuring, when directed at someone who is considered to be a friend or who has been helpful in the past, is an indication of a lack of appreciation. Rather than use complaining, we should know the person well enough to trust them and not to look at some isolated incident we are not happy with, but rather at their long-term record. It is interesting that when we have helped some people over and over again, if we cannot do it once for some reason or other, they try to make us look like the worst people on the face of the earth.

Some of God's worst judgments came down upon the people of Israel because of their complaining and murmuring.

There is a proper way to look at such a result. A person who has helped you in the past did not have to extend any kindness to you in the first place, so you should appreciate the fact that he or she did—even if it was only that one time. Murmuring only makes things worse.

Murmuring is an indication of lack of trust and implies negative and sinister characteristics on the part of the person against whom the murmuring is directed. The murmurer feels that if he does not murmur and complain, he will not obtain the assistance he needs. But the prior assistance received did not come as a result of complaints, but rather because of the love and kindness of a benefactor. And if love provided the first favor, then one need not complain to obtain future favors.

Since we know how offensive murmuring and complaining is to us, it should cause us to think twice before ever murmuring and complaining against God. Murmuring hinders His work and His ability to bless us. Things would often be different if a person had not opened his or her mouth negatively.

Some of God's worst judgments came down upon the people of Israel because of their complaining and murmuring. God had done so much for them, and their leaders, Moses and Aaron, had done so much for them too, sacrificing their very lives for them. Still, every time they had a chance, it seemed, they found something to murmur and complain about.

In this case, the occasion of their dissatisfaction was a declining food supply. That was a problem, but they should have known that the same God who had provided for them in the past would again supply their every need. He had lovingly made ways for them in the past, and He would do it again.

When they complained, however, God mysteriously did what He was probably going to do anyway; He sent manna, or heavenly bread, into their camp to feed them. This manna was something wonderful indeed and was described in this way: *"like wafers made with honey"* (Exodus 16:31). That sounds awfully good to me. Manna was apparently the ultimate health bar. It was nutritionally adequate, and it also seemed to have medicinal qualities.

The manna was miraculous. It fell only six days each week. It never fell on the Sabbath, and this continued to occur over the long space of forty years. Then, just as suddenly as it had started, it stopped. The people had now arrived at the Promised Land and would have other means of supplying their needed food.

When any of the people took more of the manna than was allotted to them or tried to accumulate it, it would spoil and breed worms. They could not store it overnight—except on the sixth day. Then they kept an extra day's supply so that on the Sabbath they could dedicate themselves to worshiping God. It this case, the extra manna did not spoil. If you are faithful to worship God, He will preserve what is yours.

On any other day, when they tried to keep the manna, it spoiled. This forced the people to rely on God every day, because without a miracle from Him, they would not have had anything to eat. He gave them a one-day supply everyday, except the sixth day, when He gave them a two-day supply. Don't expect God to supply for you months and years ahead of time. He loves for you to trust Him, so He does it a day at a time, a week at a time, or a month at a time.

Even Jesus taught us to pray:

Give us this day our daily bread. Matthew 6:11

Having only enough for the day forces us to continually rely on our Lord. Every evening, when the children of Israel went to bed, they did so with empty cupboards. They had to look up to heaven and say, "Lord, if You don't do a miracle for us tomorrow, we cannot go on living." This daily sense of dependance upon the Lord was healthy for them, and it will be healthy for you too.

The manna was so miraculous that Moses commanded the people to keep some of it as a memorial to God's goodness. It was to be part of their testimony. Some of the miracle manna was collected, put into a golden pot, and placed inside the Ark of the Covenant. There it reminded the people of the great miracle God had done for them every day in the wilderness and of His promise to supply their needs always.

AARON'S ROD THAT BUDDED

The second item kept in the Ark of the Covenant was Aaron's rod. As we will discuss in more detail in a later chapter of the book, at one point Moses and Aaron encountered some very severe opposition. A man named Korah gathered around himself two hundred and fifty respected men of the community, and together they confronted their leaders:

> *Now Korah the son of Izhar, the son of Kohath, the son of Levi, with Dathan and Abiram the sons of Eliab, and On the son of Peleth, sons of Reuben, took men; and they rose up before Moses with some of the children of Israel, two hundred and fifty leaders of the congregation, representatives of the congregation, men of renown. They gathered together against Moses and Aaron, and said to them, "You take too much upon yourselves, for all the congregation is holy, every one of them, and the Lord is among them. Why then do you exalt yourselves above the congregation of the Lord?"* Numbers 16:1-3

Moses listened to this complaint very seriously, and it affected him deeply. He fell on his face before God and asked how he should respond. In the end, he answered Korah and his company:

"Tomorrow morning the Lord will show who is His and who is holy, and will cause him to come near to Him. That one whom He chooses He will cause to come near to Him." Numbers 16:5

As Moses prayed further about this very serious matter, God showed him that judgement must come upon the rebels and that he should warn others not to partake of their sin. He did this. Then he called Korah and boldly predicted that judgment would soon come upon him and his family, concluding:

"By this you shall know that the Lord has sent me to do all these works, for I have not done them of my own will." Numbers 16:28

And God backed Moses up:

Then it came to pass, as he finished speaking all these words, that the ground split apart under them, and the earth opened its mouth and swallowed them up, with their households and all the men with Korah, with all their goods.

And a fire came out from the Lord and consumed the two hundred and fifty men who were offering incense. Numbers 16:31-32 and 35

But not everyone was pleased with this turn of events. The rest of the people decided to complain about how this whole affair had been handled, and, thus, to challenge further Moses and his leadership:

On the next day all the congregation of the children of Israel murmured against Moses and Aaron, saying, "You have killed the people of the Lord." Numbers 16:41

At this point, God was angry—very angry:

Now it happened, when the congregation had gathered against Moses and Aaron, that they turned toward the tabernacle of meeting; and suddenly the cloud covered it, and the glory of the Lord appeared.

And the Lord spoke to Moses, saying, "Get away from among this congregation, that I may consume them in a moment." And they fell on their faces.

Now those who died in the plague were fourteen thousand seven hundred, besides those who died in the Korah incident. Numbers 16:42, 44-45 and 49

This was still not the end of the matter. God wanted to settle this thing once and for all, so He ordered Moses to bring twelve rods, one from each tribe of Israel, and to put the name of the head of each tribe on one of the rods. He was to place Aaron's name on one of them, representing the sons of Levi. God would give a miraculous sign showing which of the men He had chosen to lead the people. And He could choose whomever He wanted.

Moses was further ordered:

"Then you shall place them [the twelve rods] *in the tabernacle of meeting before the Testimony, where I meet with you. And it shall be that the rod of the man whom I choose will blossom; thus I will rid Myself of the complaints of the children of Israel, which they make against you."* Numbers 17:4-5

I believe that Moses and Aaron slept well that night. They knew that God was working for them, and what they discovered in the Tabernacle the next day proved it:

Now it came to pass on the next day that Moses went into the tabernacle of witness, and behold, the rod of Aaron, of the house of Levi, had sprouted and put forth buds, had produced blossoms and yielded ripe almonds. Then Moses brought out all the rods from before the Lord to all the children of Israel; and they looked, and each man took his rod. And the Lord said to Moses, "Bring Aaron's rod back before the Testimony, to be kept as a sign against the rebels, that you may put their complaints away from Me, lest they die."

Thus did Moses; just as the Lord had commanded him, so he did.
Numbers 17:8-11

As each of the first eleven men picked up his rod and examined it, he could see no difference in it. It had been a dry stick the night before, and it was still a dry stick. But with Aaron's rod, there *was* a difference. And *what* a difference! Aaron's rod, which had been as the others the night before, little more than a dry stick, had now budded and blossomed and brought forth fully developed fruit. And it had done all that in a single night.

Many of the people had been against Aaron, but God had taken his side. When God chooses you, there is nothing any man or woman can say or do about it.

David had enemies on every side too, and they did everything they could to try to block him and stop his forward progress. They looked down on him and gave a thumbs down to everything he tried to do, but the Lord surprised them all. David sang:

You prepare a table before me in the presence of my enemies. Psalm 23:5

God stepped up with a napkin over His arm and served David up a helping of blessing in the sight of all of his enemies. "Sit down," He said to David. "I want all of your enemies to see this." And He proceeded to serve His child as they watched.

When you are chosen by God to lead, He will bless you even when others don't like you. He will lift you up even when everyone else is trying to push you down.

That Aaron's rod would bud, blossom, and bear fruit is an assurance that God can bring dead things back to life. If anything has died in your world, submit it to His miracle-working power.

If your marriage is in trouble, if your doctor has given you a bad diagnosis, or if your boss is not happy with you, and your days on the job seem to be numbered, look up to the God of Aaron. If God could

If God could make a dead stick bring forth in one night, He can turn your situation around too.

꧁꧂

make a dead stick bring forth in one night, He can turn your situation around too.

Even Jesus died. He did it for us, but God brought Him back to life. Now He has the keys of death, and He offers life to you today. If He can unlock death, He can unlock anything else that seems to threaten you. No wonder the rod of Aaron was placed in the Ark as a permanent testimony! It was a reminder that when God is on our side, who can be against us?

THE TWO STONE TABLETS FROM MORIAH

God gave Moses the Ten Commandments written by His own finger on two tablets, or tables, of stone. Moses had been on the mountain for forty days and nights, and he was so happy to be coming back down carrying those miracle stones with him, for he just knew that the people would all be very blessed by what was written on them. Every society needs laws and order for continuity, and the laws on these stones had been given by God Himself. What joy Moses felt in his heart in that moment!

But, alas, as Moses arrived at the bottom of the mountain, he was very disturbed to find the people drunken and worshipping an idol. He was so incensed with this display of disdain for the greatness and holiness of God that he threw the tablets of stone to the ground and broke them. Then he set about to destroy the idol the people were worshipping. Because of their sin, the Lord sent a plague upon the people (see Exodus 32:35).

Moses made intercession for the people, and ultimately God forgave them and gave them a second chance. Moses remembered it this way:

At that time the Lord said to me, "Hew for yourself two tablets of stone like the first, and come up to Me on the mountain and make

yourself an ark of wood. And I will write on the tablets the words that were on the first tablets, which you broke; and you shall put them in the ark." So I made an ark of acacia wood, hewed two tablets of stone like the first, and went up the mountain, having the two tablets in my hand. And He wrote on the tablets according to the first writing, the Ten Commandments, which the Lord had spoken to you in the mountain from the midst of the fire in the day of the assembly; and the Lord gave them to me. Then I turned and came down from the mountain, and put the tablets in the ark which I had made; and there they are, just as the Lord commanded me.
Deuteronomy 10:1-5

These tablets contained God's commandments for His people, His will regarding their behavior, and the fact that they were kept in the Ark was proof that God had given them a second chance. Despite the fact that they had "messed up," God had been merciful to them, and had done the same miracle for them all over again—writing His laws on another set of stone tablets.

No wonder this second set of stone tablets was kept in the Ark of the Convent. It was a perpetual memorial to the fact that God is merciful and loving and readily gives a second chance to those who seek Him.

THE TESTIMONY

The Ark of the Covenant was sometimes called the Ark of Testimony. On the outside it was the Ark of the Covenant, but on the inside it was the Ark of Testimony because what was in there was a testimony to the people of Israel (and to their neighbors) that God was good, that He was good TO THEM, and that He was good to them NOW. And just as the Ark and its contents was a testimony for Israel then, it is a testimony for us today. God hasn't changed, and He is still doing miracles for His people. His Word declares:

But my God shall supply all your need according to His riches in glory, by Christ Jesus. Philippians 4:19, KJV

You need a pot of manna in your testimony so that you'll always know that it is so.

You need a rod that has budded in your testimony. Then, when people try to block you and hold you back, you will know that God is on your side. As the psalmist declared:

When my father and my mother forsake me, then the Lord will take care of me. Psalm 27:10

As Paul wrote to the Romans:

What then shall we say to these things? If God is for us, who can be against us? Romans 8:31

As the prophet Jeremiah declared:

For I know the thoughts that I think toward you, says the Lord, thoughts of peace and not of evil, to give you a future and a hope. Jeremiah 29:11

And as Jesus said:

You did not choose Me, but I chose you and appointed you that you should go and bear fruit, and that your fruit should remain, that whatever you ask the Father in My name He may give you. John 15:16

Let there be a budding, blossoming, fruit-producing rod in your testimony from now on.

Let their be a second set of stone tablets in your testimony as well, indicating that God has given you a second chance. For some, it's not a second, a third or even a fourth chance. God has given some a tenth chance, to others a twenty-fifth chance, and to still others even more. He is a loving and merciful God. He said:

"Come now, and let us reason together, ...though your sins are like scarlet, they shall be as white as snow; though they are red like crimson, they shall be as wool." Isaiah 1:18

Please keep a second set of stone tablets in your Ark, and let that be your testimony. Then learn to give it forcefully and boldly.

TWO IMPORTANT THINGS TO EXPECT FOR YOUR TESTIMONY

There were two important things accomplished through the testimony of the Ark. (1.) The people sent their testimony into the future:

So they departed from the mountain of the Lord on a journey of three days; and the ark of the covenant of the Lord went before them for the three days' journey, to search out a resting place for them. And the cloud of the Lord was above them by day when they went out from the camp. So it was, whenever the ark set out, that Moses said:

"Rise up, O Lord! Let Your enemies be scattered, and let those who hate You flee before You." And when it rested, he said: "Return, O Lord, to the many thousands of Israel." Numbers 10:33-36

The testimony was sent ahead, and when the people arrived, the testimony had already done its work. Let God's faithfulness in the past determine your future. He hasn't changed, and He will somehow make a way for you. He who has begun a good work in you will surely continue it, and He will surely finish it:

Being confident of this very thing, that He who has begun a good work in you will complete it until the day of Jesus Christ. Philippians 1:6

The same God who blessed you in the past will take you into your future. As John Newton, the ex-slave trader, penned: "'Tis grace that brought me safe thus far, and grace will see me through." Send your testimony into the future.

The same God who did a miracle for you yesterday will do a miracle for you today and tomorrow, and the same God who forgave you in the past will forgive you today and tomorrow as well.

The people of Israel went even further. Not only were they able to send their testimony into the future, but (2.) They were able to send their testimony into the impossible:

So it was, when the people set out from their camp to cross over the Jordan, with the priests bearing the ark of the covenant before the people, and as those who bore the ark came to the Jordan, and the feet of the priests who bore the ark dipped in the edge of the water (for the Jordan overflows all its banks during the whole time of harvest), that the waters which came down from upstream stood still, and rose in a heap very far away at Adam, the city that is beside Zaretan. So the waters that went down into the Sea of the Arabah, the Salt Sea, failed, and were cut off; and the people crossed over opposite Jericho. Then the priests who bore the ark of the covenant of the Lord stood firm on dry ground in the midst of the Jordan; and all Israel crossed over on dry ground, until all the people had crossed completely over the Jordan. Joshua 3:14-17

When they arrived at the Jordan River, they found the water to be uncrossable. What should they do? God told Joshua to send their testimony into the impossible.

The priests took up the Ark and began to advance toward the flooded waters of the Jordan. The moment their feet touched the water, the troubled waters recognized the testimony and began backing up, so that the children of Israel could then cross over on dry land.

Child of God, the same God who brought you safe thus far is still alive, and He is still able. As the popular song asks?

> *Got any rivers you think are uncrossable?*
> *Got any mountains you can't tunnel through?*
> *God specializes in things thought impossible.*
> *And He can do what no other power can do.*

Boldly send your testimony into some impossible situation, and just watch what God will do with it.

MAKING THE NECESSARY EFFORT

It may surprise some to know that not everything will be served to us on a silver platter. Although the manna was miraculous, the people had to work to gather it. This had to be done early in the morning, and if they delayed until later in the day, the manna would melt and disappear, and their blessing would be lost. After they had gathered the manna, the people then had to prepare it. Why is it that so many seem to be lying back expecting God to serve them breakfast in bed?

You will not experience your divine encounter without putting forth some effort and doing something that will touch the heart of God. This "something" is represented by the furnishing in the Tabernacle. They represent steps toward encounter with God, steps to finding the pathway to His presence. If you will follow them, I can assure you that the experience you so desperately desire *will* come.

Chapter Nine

THE MERCY SEAT
YOU CAN COME NOW

You shall put the mercy seat on top of the ark, and in the ark you shall put the Testimony that I will give you. And there I will meet with you, and I will speak with you from above the mercy seat, from between the two cherubim which are on the ark of the Testimony, about everything which I will give you in commandment to the children of Israel. Exodus 25:21-22

The way has been made, and you can now come to the Mercy Seat, the place of the fullness of God's presence.

We have established the fact that God is holy, jealous, just, loving, merciful, and forgiving—among other things. For a little while, let us revisit His holiness:

Who is like You, O Lord, among the gods? Who is like You, glorious in holiness, fearful in praises, doing wonders? Exodus 15:11

God's very name is Holy:

For thus says the High and Lofty One Who inhabits eternity, whose name is Holy: "I dwell in the high and holy place." Isaiah 57:15

As I stated in a previous chapter, the Hebrew word used to indicate God's holiness refers to His absoluteness, majesty, and awfulness (or awesomeness) in comparison to us. He is to be reverenced and venerated as totally separate from all that is human and earthly. This term *holiness,* when used in relationship to God, denotes His essential and absolute moral perfection.

As we said at the outset, who a person is and what a person is, in many cases, determines how that person is dealt with, or at least how they *should* be dealt with. For instance, if you value your life, you would not just go running up to the President of the United States of America. As our President, he is to be treated with respect, and he has around him men and women who assure that he is properly treated.

Some people have no respect or regard for anybody. They always seem to be up in somebody's face. But, sooner or later, they get in the wrong person's face, and then they reap the fruit of their actions and attitude.

Sometimes, the nicer you try to be to people, the more likely it is that they will feel they can disrespect you and speak to you and of you in a demeaning way. This spirit of disrespect can even invade the Church, where God has instituted a divine order:

And I will give you shepherds according to My heart, who will feed you with knowledge and understanding. Jeremiah 3:15

Let the elders who rule well be counted worthy of double honor, especially those who labor in the word and doctrine. 1 Timothy 5:17

Obey those who rule over you, and be submissive, for they watch out for your souls, as those who must give account. Let them do so with joy and not with grief, for that would be unprofitable for you. Hebrews 13:17 our concept of who and what pastors are will determine how you deal with them. It would be much better for us if we could adjust our attitudes to the clear teachings of the Word of God.

In a similar way, our concept of who God is and what He is like has a great impact on how we deal with Him. And how we deal with Him affects our personal well-being in every way. If God was to be the God of the Israelites, they would have to recognize and trust in His awesome power and might. They would need to respect and honor Him for who He was.

You don't just walk up to Most High and holy God and start a conversation and establish a relationship with Him. Because He is the holy God, He must be approached according to the instructions which He has left to us. There are examples in the Bible that should cause us all to think twice about this matter. One of them that we already looked at in this book was the case of Nadab and Abihu. They failed to obey God and were struck dead.

As we have seen, God even demanded the respect of Moses, and He demanded the respect of the priests Moses put into place. It has never paid to fool around with God, and recognition of and respect for God's holiness has always been an essential ingredient of effective worship. In the time of the Tabernacle, precise conformity to the standards and procedures outlined by God and His leader Moses was not only required, but was enforced under threat of death.

The entire dispensation of Law required total obedience:

When your son asks you in time to come, saying, "What is the meaning of the testimonies, the statutes, and the judgments which the Lord our God has commanded you?" then you shall say to your son: "We were slaves of Pharaoh in Egypt, and the Lord brought us out of Egypt with a mighty hand; and the Lord showed signs and wonders before our eyes, great and severe, against Egypt, Pharaoh, and all his household. Then He brought us out from there, that He might bring us in, to give us the land of which He swore to our fathers.

And the Lord commanded us to observe all these statutes, to fear the Lord our God, for our good always, that He might preserve us alive, as it is this day. Then it will be righteousness for us, if we are careful to observe all these commandments before the Lord our God, as He has commanded us." Deuteronomy 6:20-25

Unfortunately, this requirement of righteousness was at a level that the people of Moses' day could not reach. The very existence of the Tabernacle itself was an indication on God's part that there would be sins and failures among the people. Its structure and its furnishings assumed this sinfulness and moral inadequacy.

The Bronze Altar, with its sacrifices, represented God's selection of an acceptable price to be paid so that sin could be forgiven. Since no earthly sacrifice is perfect, in another sense, it also represented the future sacrifice to be made by Jesus Himself.

The Bronze Laver, or Basin, at which the priests would wash their hands, feet, and (at times) other parts of their bodies, represented moral and spiritual cleansing, and it was to be used often.

The Table of Showbread represented God's people constantly before His presence, offering themselves to Him.

The Candlestick represented moral and spiritual light, the light that God and His people were to be in a dark world.

The Golden Altar of Incense and the sweet smoke that ascended from it represented what God's people and their worship were to God—a sweet aroma. The smoke of the incense represented their prayers and their worship.

The Mercy Seat, known in the New Testament book of Hebrews as the Throne of Grace, sat over the Ark of the Covenant in the Most Holy Place, or Holy of Holies, and represented the culmination of, and the success of the process of involvement in each of the other areas of the Tabernacle. Everything the people did in the Tabernacle led them to the Mercy Seat. The Mercy Seat represented the presence of God and the believers' communion with Him. And you can come to the Mercy Seat now.

THE TOTAL INADEQUACY OF THE LAW

The dispensation of the Law and, with it, the Tabernacle, was inadequate, restrictive, and filled with fear, insecurity, and apprehension. It was not God's best. This is why the Bible says that it was merely a type, or shadow, of what was to come.

The Tabernacle was inadequate because each of its various ceremonies had to be performed over and over again. Every morning and every evening sacrifices had to be offered. Every year, on the Day of Atonement, the High Priest had to go through elaborate rituals and sacrifices to atone for the sins of the people. And when they ministered in the Tabernacle, the priests had to go to the Laver again and again to wash.

The era of the Tabernacle was restrictive because Gentiles were not even permitted to enter its Outer Court. They could never go to the place of sacrifice and washing. Only the Israelites were allowed into the Outer Court.

Even those who were descendants of eleven of the twelve tribes of Israel were restricted. They could go into the Court of the Tabernacle but never to the inner areas. So, if you were from any tribe other than Levi this was as far as you could go.

Even the tribe of Levi was restricted. It was not the whole tribe that could enter, but only those who served as priests. At the time of Moses, this meant that only the four sons of Aaron could go into the Holy Place, along with their father and their Uncle Moses.

These priests were also restricted. They could go into the Holy Place, but never into the Most Holy Place. Only the High Priest could go there—Aaron himself at the time (and Moses).

Aaron, too, was restricted. He could not go into the Most Holy Place every day or whenever he chose to go there. He could go there only once a year, and then on a very specific day—the Day of Atonement.

There were other restrictions. Anyone having a physical blemish or deformity was automatically denied entry to the Tabernacle—no matter what tribe he or she belonged to.

The Tabernacle era was filled with fear, insecurity, and apprehension. Failure to precisely obey all the instructions regarding Tabernacle worship could result in immediate death. As innocent animals were sacrificed upon the altar, the priests were reminded that they and the people they served were really the ones who should have suffered execution and death on the altar—because of their sins.

Everything in the Tabernacle had to have the blood of the sacrifice placed upon it, as an "atonement" for its inadequacy. This was true of the priests themselves. And the high priest, before he could go into the Holy of Holies, had to have the blood applied to his right ear, his right thumb, and his right big toe. If this was not done, and he went into the Holy of Holies anyway, he would be destroyed.

After doing everything he knew to do to be clean, the High Priest still had to take other precautions. Into the hem of his garment, tiny bells were sown so that others would know whether or not he was still alive as he went about his duties in the Holy of Holies. Before he went in, a rope was attached to his body so that he could be pulled out if God chose to strike him dead. Even under those dire circumstances, no one would be permitted to go in and bring out his body.

As we noted, there was a huge veil, a curtain, in the Tabernacle, which hung between the Holy Place and the Most Holy Place, dividing those two spaces. This veil not only separated the priests from the Ark of the Covenant and the Most Holy Place; it prevented them from even looking into the Most Holy Place.

This represented the relationship between God and His people. He was drawn to them by His love for them, but He was also driven from them by their sinfulness and inadequacy. The people, too, were drawn to God by their need for fellowship with Him, but they were also driven from Him by their fear and their wickedness. The only remedy available for them was the sacrifice of blood:

> *For the life of the flesh is in the blood, and I have given it to you upon the altar to make atonement for your souls; for it is the blood that makes atonement for the soul.* Leviticus 17:11

And according to the law almost all things are purified with blood,
and without shedding of blood there is no remission. Hebrews 9:22

Then there was the yearly Day of Atonement.

THE YEARLY DAY OF ATONEMENT

The term *atonement* refers to the covering or canceling of sin and has the effect of bringing God and that which is separated from Him together (at-one-ment). The Day of Atonement, the day of cancellation of sin, was not only for the atonement of the High Priest, the other priests, and the people to God; it was also for the atonement of the Tabernacle, the Altar, and the Holy Place itself. The reason given for this was that the Tabernacle remained *"among them in the midst of their uncleanness"* (Leviticus 16:16). The sins of the people were so displeasing to God that even the Tabernacle had to be atoned for—because of its contact with *them*. Only through the ceremonies of the Day of Atonement could it continue to serve as a place of worship and sacrifice.

On that important day, the High Priest was required to wash himself and put on plain linen clothing appointed for the special ceremonies he would perform. After slaying a bullock as a sin offering for himself and his family, he was to carry incense into the Holy of Holies and allow it to burn until smoke filled the room. After this, he was to return with the blood from his sin offering and sprinkle it to the east of the altar and then seven times before the altar.

A goat was also sacrificed as a sin offering unto the Lord, and the same thing was done with the blood of this offering. Afterward the remaining blood was to be placed on the horns, or handles, of the Altar of Burnt Offering and sprinkled seven times upon it. Thus, the Tabernacle was made acceptable for another year as the meeting place of God and His people.

After this, another goat, would be brought before the High Priest. Laying his hands on the head of the goat, he would confess his sins and the sins of the people. Thus, in theory, his and their sins passed to the goat.

The blood of animals could not bring about a permanent sense of the presence and power of God...

꧁꧂

Upon that goat now rested the unworthiness of the Tabernacle and the sins of the priests and the people. This animal was known as a scapegoat.

A man carefully selected for this unique purpose would then lead the scapegoat far into the wilderness, so far that it could never find its way back, and there he would release it. This was a moment of great rejoicing for the people, for the scapegoat carried their sins and the iniquities of the past year far away from them.

After washing himself, the High Priest would return to offer burnt offerings for himself and for the people.

It is difficult to conceive of the depths of emotion that must have filled this day year after year for the Jewish people. They were sorrowful and repentant and hopeful, and the High Priest was full of fear for his own life, but all of them knew that iniquity would soon rush in upon them again, and the next year, it would all have to be done over again.

The blood of animals could not relieve the conscience of man from the guilt he felt. It could not change his heart, nor his nature. And, although the sacrifices of the Tabernacle (and later the Temple) brought immediate pardon, they could not remove the power sin had over man.

SOMETHING BETTER

The blood of animals could not bring about a permanent sense of the presence and power of God, and since this was true, there was a sincere desire, on the part of both God and man, for something better. With all of the sacrifices made each year, there were not enough lambs, goats, and bullocks on the earth to atone for all the people's sins. The blood sacrifices offered by sinful men did not appease God's just nature in any way. Man's hopes were exhausted, and God's patience had reached its end. But, thank God, all of this was just a shadow of what was to come.

More than seven hundred years before the coming of Christ, Isaiah prophesied of something better to come:

He was wounded for our transgressions, He was bruised for our iniquities; the chastisement for our peace was upon Him, and by His stripes we are healed. All we like sheep have gone astray; we have turned, every one, to his own way; and the Lord has laid on Him the iniquity of us all. Isaiah 53:5-6

The prophet was seeing hundreds of years into the future, when a perfect Man would become the perfect sacrifice. For now, the people would struggle on with the inadequacy of the Law. The writer of Hebrews, again, articulated God's final verdict on the sacrificial system of the Tabernacle:

For it is not possible that the blood of bulls and goats could take away sins. Hebrews 10:4

The Tabernacle, with the best it could offer, was a failure. God needed to intervene personally for man, for no earthly sacrifice was found worthy to redeem him.

As we have seen, we needed someone related to us, for it was not seemly that an innocent animal should die for the sins of a man. We needed someone who was worthy, for this would not be the death of one man for another, but the death of one man for all men of all times. And we needed someone who was innocent. Otherwise the one sacrificed would have been suffering and dying for his own sins. Jesus, the Son of God, met of all these conditions.

We walked beside Him from judgment hall to judgment hall. And, as He was tried, we were on trial for every sin of our lives. We had to nod our heads in agreement when the verdict was guilty and the sentence was death.

We walked beside Him to the hill called Calvary, and there our sins hung Jesus on the cross. They drove the nails into His hands and feet, crushed the thorns into his skull, and caused His blood to flow down from the cross. It was our sins that caused Him to cry out in agony. John Mark recorded the scene:

And Jesus cried out with a loud voice, and breathed His last. Mark 15:37

THE WAY IS OPENED

In that moment, something wonderful happened:

Then the veil of the temple was torn in two from top to bottom. So when the centurion, who stood opposite Him, saw that He cried out like this and breathed His last, he said, "Truly this Man was the Son of God!" Mark 15:38-39

The Veil had been destroyed, and a way had been opened into the very presence of God. The people were surprised to find that the Veil had been torn *"from top to bottom."* If it had been torn from the bottom to the top or from one side to the other, we might think that men had done it. But it was torn from the top to the bottom, showing that the Omnipotent God Himself had reached down and opened a way for us into His throne room. Now hear the Lord call:

Whosoever will, let him take the water of life freely. Revelation 22:17, KJV

Jesus, our great High Priest, had made the ultimate sacrifice for us, and had done for us what no Old Testament sacrifice could do:

Seeing then that we have a great High Priest who has passed through the heavens, Jesus the Son of God, let us hold fast our confession. For we do not have a High Priest who cannot sympathize with our weaknesses, but was in all points tempted as we are, yet without sin.

Let us therefore come boldly to the throne of grace [the Mercy Seat], that we may obtain mercy and find grace to help in time of need. Hebrews 4:14-16

The King James Version of the Bible says it this way:

For we have not an high priest which cannot be touched with the feeling of our infirmities; but was in all points tempted like as we are, yet without sin.

Jesus can be *"touched."* Have you ever known people who seemed to be completely beyond being touched, so haughty, arrogant, and nonchalant that you just couldn't get through to them? No matter what you did or said, they remained remote, and distant, considering themselves to be so much better than everyone else around them that they simply could not be bothered. Such a person cannot be touched by anything or anybody.

I've known people who could actually laugh at those who were suffering and poke fun at those who were infirm, those who could condemn and reject those whose sins were different from their own. There are even those who can turn their backs on the needy and feel no remorse.

People like that cannot be touched, but I'm so glad that Jesus is not like them. He *can* be touched, and He *is* touched by the feeling of our infirmities. He is so easily touched that He wept at the grave of Lazarus. He cares more for us than we do for ourselves. While the inhabitants of Jerusalem were carefree and happy in their wickedness, Jesus was touched by their plight and was weeping over them:

O Jerusalem, Jerusalem, thou that killest the prophets, and stonest them which are sent unto thee, how often would I have gathered thy children together, even as a hen gathereth her chickens under her wings, and ye would not! Matthew 23:37, KJV

Jesus can be touched. The woman with the issue of blood, who had been rejected by everybody else, was able to touch Him. And no matter who you are or what you have done, you can touch Him too.

167

He is *"touched with the feeling of our infirmities,"* meaning that He is aware of and sympathizes with what we suffer. Some of you are troubled and confused. Some of you are confronted by insurmountable barriers that keep you in or keep you out. Maybe you have told no one about your problems. Maybe you have been afraid to even pray about them. But I want you to know that Jesus is already touched by them. His heart already goes out to you, and His eyes of compassion are looking upon you even now.

Not only can Jesus be touched, but He was also *"tempted in all points, like as we are, yet without sin."* He walked the road that you're walking, and Satan tried to make Him sin. He was not only tempted, He was tempted *"in all points,"* or in every way. He received not just a few temptations, but every temptation known to man.

The fact that He was tempted in all points as we are lets us know that His temptations were not mild. They were not easy. They were just like ours. But He went through all of His temptations without committing even one sin.

Don't ever believe that your temptations are unique:

No temptation has overtaken you except such as is common to man; but God is faithful, who will not allow you to be tempted beyond what you are able, but with the temptation will also make the way of escape, that you may be able to bear it. 1 Corinthians 10:13

When I experience a problem, it is always consoling to me to know that someone else has experienced the same problem before me. Such people seem to really understand what I am now going through. Others have a habit of saying, "I understand" in those moments, but the truth is that unless they have had the same experience, they really *cannot* understand. Jesus really knows, and He really understands because He traveled this way before us.

As our High Priest, Advocate, and Mediator, Jesus stands between earth and heaven to plead our case before God the Father. Although we are sinners, God hears us and forgives us because Jesus has paid the price for our sins in His blood. This is why we make our prayers in the name of Jesus. He has a limitless credit line in the Bank of Heaven. Although I have no funds on deposit there, Jesus has given me a book of checks signed in His blood, and whatever I need, He has already authorized it.

Forgiveness is available in His name. Healing is available in His name. Deliverance is available in His name. Power is available in His name. Whatever you need is available in His name.

This is why the biblical writer could say, *"Therefore ..."* (Hebrews 4:16). What is this *"therefore"*? It is the logical conclusion of what Jesus has done. Because of what He has done, we can come to the throne of grace. Because of what He has done, we can come boldly before God. Because of what He has done, we can obtain mercy and find grace to help in time of need.

In Jesus, not only will you find one who can be touched, and not only will

In Jesus, not only will you find one who can be touched, and not only will you find one who has been tempted as you are, but you will also find one who is merciful.

you find one who has been tempted as you are, but you will also find one who is merciful. The old hymn of the Church, *He Lifted Me* (also known as *In Loving Kindness Jesus Came*), Charles H. Gabriel (1856-1932) proclaimed in 1905:

> *In lovingkindness Jesus came my soul in mercy to reclaim*
> *And from the depths of sin and shame thru grace He lifted me.*

Chorus:
From sinking sand He lifted me

ENCOUNTERING GOD

With tender hand He lifted me;
From shades of night to plains of light
O praise His name, He lifted me!

When you go to Him, not only will you find mercy; you will also find grace to help in the time of need. Many people seem to want to help us when we don't really need their help. Then, when we *do* need them, they're nowhere to be found. Jesus is always there at our time of need. In 1855 Joseph Scriven (1819-1886) wrote the blessed words:

What a Friend we have in Jesus, all our sins and griefs to bear!
What a privilege to carry everything to God in prayer!
O what peace we often forfeit, O what needless pain we bear,
All because we do not carry everything to God in prayer.

Jesus can help you today. He has opened the way into the Holy of Holies and has given you access to the Mercy Seat.

YOUR PERSONAL COMMITMENT

Before I close this book, I must ask a question of you. If this were the last day of your life here on earth, would you be ready for eternity? Could you stand before God with your head held high? Are your sins forgiven? Do you know Jesus as your Lord and Savior? Do you have the peace and fulfillment that only He can give?

Jesus died for your sins and arose again so that you might have life and have it more abundantly. If you don't have that life today, I want to offer here a prayer for your soul.

Right where you are today, you can be saved and begin your walk toward the Holy of Holies. It has all been made possible through the precious blood sacrificed by Jesus, and every sin you have ever committed can be forgiven today. Tell God that you're ready for it right now as I pray for you.

Dear Lord,

I pray for all those who wish to come to You today. Right now, forgive every sin in their lives, and draw them to Yourself. Set them free from sin so that they will never again be the same.

Amen!

Now you pray a prayer with me, and mean it from your heart:

Dear Lord,

I'm sorry for my sins.

Please forgive me for the wrong I've done and the wrong I've been.

I want to be saved.

I believe that Jesus is the Son of God and that He died for my sins.

I also believe that He rose again from the dead.

And I accept Him today as my Lord and Savior.

I give my life to Him.

I thank You, Lord, for forgiving my sins, for saving my soul, and for changing my life.

Now thank Him because every sin *is* forgiven. The blood of Jesus Christ has washed you and made you free.

The Bible states emphatically:

If you confess with your mouth the Lord Jesus and believe in your heart that God has raised Him from the dead, you will be saved. For with the heart one believes unto righteousness, and with the mouth confession is made unto salvation. For the Scripture says, "Whoever believes on Him will not be put to shame." For there is no distinction between Jew and Greek, for the same Lord over all is rich to all who call upon Him. For "whoever calls on the name of the Lord shall be saved." Romans 10:9-13

The Tabernacle was called the Tabernacle of meeting because its purpose was to cause a meeting between God and man. God wanted to meet with His people, and that's still true today. He loves YOU and wants to be part of your everyday life. And, just as God gave the Israelites a definite pattern for the building of the Tabernacle, He wants to give you a definite pattern for your life from this day forth. This is not to restrict you, but so that you can find and walk in His way.

The role of the Tabernacle, with its Brazen Altar, Bronze Laver, Table of Showbread, Golden Lampstand, Altar of Incense, and the Ark of the Covenant and the accompanying Mercy Seat were all completed and brought to an end by the sacrifice of Jesus Christ, God's Son:

And every priest stands ministering daily and offering repeatedly the same sacrifices, which can never take away sins. But this Man, after He had offered one sacrifice for sins forever, sat down at the right hand of God, from that time waiting till His enemies are made His footstool. For by one offering He has perfected forever those who are being sanctified. Hebrews 10:11-14

For when we were still without strength, in due time Christ died for the ungodly. For scarcely for a righteous man will one die; yet perhaps for a good man someone would even dare to die. But God demonstrates His own love toward us, in that while we were still sinners, Christ died for us. Romans 5:6-8

Now, we no longer need to be cleansed at the Bronze Laver; our cleansing comes through Christ and through His Word.

Husbands, love your wives, just as Christ also loved the church and gave Himself for her, that He might sanctify and cleanse her with the washing of water by the word, that He might present her to

Himself a glorious church, not having spot or wrinkle or any such thing, but that she should be holy and without blemish.
Ephesians 5:25-27

God's plan is to present us to the Father a *"glorious church, not having spot or wrinkle or any such thing."* He wants us to be like Him, *"holy and without blemish."* The only way this can be accomplished is through divine encounter. Let God draw you closer to Himself today. Discover the pathway to His presence.

Amen!